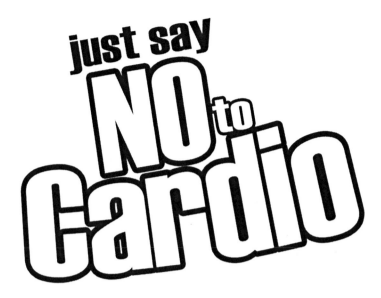

just say NO to Cardio

**Burn Belly Fat in
Half the Time Using
Research Proven
Turbulence Training**

Craig Ballantyne

Advantage®

Published by Advantage, Charleston, South Carolina.
Member of Advantage Media Group.

ADVANTAGE is a registered trademark and the Advantage colophon is a trademark of Advantage Media Group, Inc.

Printed in the United States of America.

ISBN: 978-1-59932-081-6
LCCN: 2008936314

Most Advantage Media Group titles are available at special quantity discounts for bulk purchases for sales promotions, premiums, fundraising, and educational use. Special versions or book excerpts can also be created to fit specific needs.

For more information, please write: Special Markets, Advantage Media Group, P.O. Box 272, Charleston, SC 29402 or call 1.866.775.1696.

Table of Contents

Chapter One:
The Evolution of Weight Loss

If you want to finally lose fat and stop wasting so much time doing useless cardio exercise, then I have great news for you, because you are about to discover why shorter, more intense workouts are the secret for fat burning success.

In the past, you were probably told that in order to burn fat, you had to do slow, boring cardio and maybe even lift light weights to tone your muscles. But after months of 90-minute workouts using this archaic marathon exercise system, its unlikely that you got the results you deserved.

Fortunately, in the late 1990s, exciting research was discovered that shows a short-burst exercise system called interval training actually works better than longer cardio workouts for fat burning. Plus, a landmark study from 2001 revealed that doing more intense strength training helped burn more calories after exercise when compared to lighter strength training. These are the two research proven components of Turbulence Training.

All of this new scientific evidence proved that there was a better way to exercise for fat loss. In addition, this "new school" fat loss system also required less time each week – often less than half the time most people are currently exercising – to get more results and help you achieve your goals faster.

I've been training people with these fast, fun, effective workouts for over a decade, and I guarantee it will help you burn stubborn body fat and burst through any fat loss plateau. My system is called

Turbulence Training, and I want you to, "Just say NO to Cardio," and try my workout system instead.

Turbulence Training is the trademarked workout system that I developed after years of training men and women for fat loss. It is a short-burst exercise program that allows you to get maximum results in minimum time. Because it's based on studies I reviewed while earning my master's degree in exercise physiology, I promise you that Turbulence Training is the most effective fat burning program around.

When you do short burst exercise, whether it is strength training or interval training, you put what I call *turbulence* on the muscles; and just as a plane would have to burn more fuel during turbulence, the body adjusts to exercise turbulence by burning more energy to return to its normal state. After your body exercises outside of its comfort zone, it is forced to burn a lot of energy to repair your muscles and replenish the energy that was used. This may speed up the body's metabolism during recovery, burning more fat and helping you lose inches. When this happens, weight loss follows.

I started developing Turbulence Training back in 1999 when I was a graduate student in exercise physiology at McMaster University in Hamilton, Ontario, Canada. At the time, I was very busy in the laboratory, analyzing results of a study I did on the hormone supplement taken by Mark McGwire. It's called *androstenedione*, and we wanted to see if it worked to help boost testosterone levels like the supplement labels claimed. According to my study results, androstenedione, like most supplements, didn't do anything; Mark McGwire is off the hook for that one. But in the study we had guys do some very intense workouts, and the data from this helped me identify some of the most effective exercises for building muscle and burning body fat.

One of my research duties was to draw blood from the subjects who had recently exercised and taken the supplement. I would analyze this blood, oftentimes for sixteen hours per day, with only one forty-five-minute break in which I could run across to the gym and get a workout. It was only by combining what I knew about training athletes, my research, and my background in strength training that I was able to come up with a complete fat burning workout that would have me done before the end of my break.

You see, Turbulence Training was a result of not having enough time to do anything else, but it was after I started training other people with it that I started to understand just how many other benefits there are. By 2001, I had shared the training program with thousands of men and women on the Internet, and by 2003 I launched the TurbulenceTraining.com Web site complete with more training tips, a newsletter, and success stories.

In fact, since 2006 I have released a new Turbulence Training workout each month at my membership site, TTMembers.com. You can also get the original Turbulence Training for fat loss program and all the bodyweight Turbulence Training programs at my Web site, TurbulenceTraining.com. Plus, you can find out more about the powerful success stories in the Turbulence Training transformation contest at TransformationContest.com. You can even help us vote for our transformation contest winners.

Three Keys to Fat Loss

One of the biggest mistakes that people make in their training programs is that they continue to follow the same workout for extended periods of time: eight weeks, twelve weeks, and even six months. If you do the exact same workout all the time, you just can't expect to get any additional improvements after you've made the initial changes in your body. The muscles need a new stimulus on a frequent basis. To combat your body's adaptability, Turbulence Training workouts change every four weeks.

I truly believe that if you want to continue getting results, you need to continually vary your workout program. It can mean changing the number of sets or the number of repetitions per exercise. It can be lifting more or less weight. It can be reducing the duration of rest, or it can be simply changing the order of exercises in your program. So, whatever you do, make sure you have some type of **variety** in your training program to help you get maximum results in minimum time.

Intensity is another big factor in getting results, because most people train with too low of an intensity that doesn't take their bodies outside the comfort zone. It doesn't put turbulence on the muscles, and it doesn't lead to an increase in calorie burning after exercise. So while they do get a small benefit from burning some calories in the training session, if they don't workout at high enough intensity, they won't have a post-exercise metabolism boost often associated with high-intensity training workouts. Without this extra calorie burning, they won't lose body fat.

A lot of people get intensity and elevated heart rate mixed up. They are not necessarily the same, because when you do the interval training program, there are periods of recovery built in where you want your heart rate to decrease and recover. That actually fools a lot of people and makes them think they're not doing a great workout when they are. They're so used to having that heart rate elevated all the time that they think it's really important when it's not. It's just a side effect of working hard; heart rate does not dictate your fat loss. Even though we've been brainwashed into thinking that the more you do, the more fat you'll lose, too many people are frustrated with the results and end up with overuse injuries by doing too much volume.

In addition to variety and intensity, the third thing you need in a fat loss program is **change**. This differs from variety, by which I mean variation of certain aspects of an exercise, whether repetitions or the order it comes in the workout. By change, however, I mean that every four weeks you should start a new program complete with new exercises. This is what puts the turbulence in Turbulence Training. By not repeating exercises for too long, the body is constantly adjusting; and by maintaining a high intensity, you know that your body is being pushed to burn fat.

I originally created Turbulence Training for the readers of *Men's Health* magazine. But over the years I have worked with thousands of women using the Turbulence Training system, and it works just as well for both simply because women need to do more intense workouts as much as men do. In fact, one of the studies that helped me put together Turbulence Training was based on women and strength training. It found that women doing more intense resistance training had a greater increase in metabolism than lower intensity strength training. In addition, a recent study found that interval training helped women lose more fat than slow cardio. That's why Turbulence Training works just as well for women as it does for men. To give you even more proof, the winner of the first Turbulence Training transformation contest was a woman!

One of my favorite things about Turbulence Training is that any adult can use it. I've had people as young as eighteen and as old as eighty-one use the training program. Obviously, the program will be adjusted to individual fitness levels, but that's another great part of the system; it's all based on a subjective level of intensity.

It's All about Timing

Turbulence Training is based around helping busy men and women improve their bodies without interrupting their already busy lifestyles. It is designed for the person who has a two-hour round-trip commute, an eight- to ten-hour workday, and a busy family life. These people can train at either five o'clock in the morning, at lunch, or at nine at night, or maybe sometimes right after work. They don't have time to be in the gym six days per week. But if you increase the quality of the workout, you can reduce the number of workouts and the length of workouts you need to do. It's not all about the marathon mentality; you don't have to look at training as a huge component of your evening every day. It only takes three hours per week, which is less than three *percent* of the hours in a week.

Turbulence Training workouts are short because we don't waste any time just sitting around, and we've cut down on the volume of low-intensity cardio. I get a lot of e-mails from men and women who say that they're still spending ninety minutes in the gym doing thirty minutes of strength training and sixty minutes of cardio, or maybe forty-five minutes of weights and forty-five of cardio, or some permutation of both. The truth is, those ninety minutes can be condensed down into forty-five minutes if you use supersets and interval training, but we'll talk about those later.

In Turbulence Training, you can even cut time with the warm-up. Most people go into the gym thinking they have to do five minutes on a treadmill to warm-up, but Turbulence Training advocates a general bodyweight circuit that prepares your muscles and joints specifically for the training ahead. If you do five minutes on the treadmill, you're no further ahead than if you just walked into the gym. It doesn't really prepare you for anything; it just wastes valuable time. I'll talk more about the warm-up in Chapter 5.

On non-workout days, I encourage people to live an active lifestyle. You can pretty much do whatever you want; I just want to make sure you keep your butt off the couch for at least thirty minutes. The most important thing to understand about off days is that they shouldn't leave you tired and sore for the next Turbulence Training workout, nor should they slow down your recovery from the past workout. If you really love long, slow cardio, go ahead and do that on your off days. Just don't expect it to significantly increase fat loss, and also make sure you don't run into the Dark Side of cardio, which is a problem we'll discuss later. And if I still can't convince you to stay away from cardio machines, I highly recommend you do what's called cross-training, where you do a different type of exercise every time or maybe ten minutes on the elliptical, ten minutes on the treadmill, and ten minutes on the bike. I really prefer that you incorporate activity into your lifestyle instead, such as walking the dog, running errands, or playing a sport. Typically, these types of activities are more enjoyable than camping out on a treadmill anyway.

I really think there's a mental component to weight loss in that if you hate your workouts and hate the fact that they take up so much time, it can slow down your progress. If you free up three to six hours a week using the Turbulence Training system, that takes some stress off and lets you deal with work and family issues better. A lot of people just spend too much time in the gym and no longer have hobbies or activities that are fun outside of the gym. For them, it's either work, gym, or chores at home; whereas with this lifestyle, you can go from work into a fun activity and time with your family. I really believe that Turbulence Training offers everyone an opportunity to live a better lifestyle, both mentally and physically.

Probably the best thing about this program is that it's not just for "natural" athletes or those at advanced fitness levels. I've trained men weighing over three hundred pounds and women over two hundred pounds who weren't doing any exercise in the months prior to training, and they had incredible results. In my fat loss program, there is a two-week introductory stage. Before you even get into the beginner workout, you need to start with this introductory level program, which uses a lot of *bodyweight* exercises done down on the ground such as the plank and side plank for abdominals (see Chapter 6). This is for building what some people call the *core muscles*. Then you move onto hip extensions, exercise ball leg curls, and kneeling push-ups (see Chapter 5). Those exercises are the best places to start for beginners because they help to build and strengthen the muscles around the joints. You get to that later on when we get to the intermediate and advanced workouts.

A beginner should start with strength training. Regarding interval training, which is a period of short bursts of exercise followed by periods of slow recovery, I like to use this example: a beginner cardio workout would be thirty minutes on a treadmill at 3.5 miles per hour. Therefore, interval training for this beginner would simply be going up to 3.8 miles per hour on the treadmill for one minute at a time and then dropping it back down to 3.0 miles per hour for one to two minutes at a time. This would be repeated 3-6 times in an interval training workout. So you see, it doesn't have to be sprinting to qualify as interval training. It's just slightly harder than normal cardio exercise done in increments.

Sample Interval Training Workout using four intervals of 1 minute hard at a hard pace and 2 minutes easy at a recovery pace.

Minute by Minute	Type	Intensity Level	Notes
1	Warm-up	3 out of 10	
2	Warm-up	4 out of 10	
3	Warm-up	4 out of 10	
4	Warm-up	5 out of 10	
5	Warm-up	5 out of 10	
6	Hard	8 out of 10	
7	Easy	3 out of 10	
8	Easy	3 out of 10	
9	Hard	8 out of 10	
10	Easy	3 out of 10	
11	Easy	3 out of 10	
12	Hard	8 out of 10	
13	Easy	3 out of 10	
14	Easy	3 out of 10	
15	Hard	8 out of 10	
16	Cool Down	3 out of 10	
17	Cool Down	3 out of 10	
18	Cool Down	3 out of 10	
19	Cool Down	3 out of 10	
20	Cool Down	3 out of 10	
20 minutes total			

To try the Turbulence Training workouts and get access to ask me your fat loss and exercise-related questions, visit
TurbulenceTraining.com/freegift
to get your one month FREE Turbulence Training membership.

Chapter Two
The Great Cardio Scam
(or The Great Cardio Time Robbery)

People have been told for years that they need to do lots of cardio, but a lot of them aren't getting the results they want because cardio doesn't help them lose weight. What it does is burn calories—but only for the length of time they exercise. In addition, the calorie counters on exercise machines are notoriously inaccurate. They might tell you that you have burned five hundred calories when in fact you only burned four hundred—which is still a good thing, but unfortunately that's still where your calorie burning ends. Slow, boring cardio stops working when you do. With shorter, more intense exercise, not only will you burn calories, you will boost your metabolism so that you continue to lose weight even when walking to your car or pushing a cart through the grocery store.

Not only do long cardio workouts waste your time by not burning a lot of body fat, one of the biggest dangers is injuries that result from overuse. Many people start a program when they are overweight and their joints just can't take the pounding of repetitive cardio exercise. Then, these same people who were out of shape to begin with find themselves in a doctor's office being told to stop exercising. Their fat loss comes to a screeching halt because the long stints of cardio put pressure on joints that couldn't handle it, and unfortunately there aren't many ways to burn fat while sitting with your knee in a brace.

If you are in good enough health to take the pressure of repetitive cardio, then you may lose weight, but your body won't really change.

If you have to lose about forty pounds, you might lose ten or twenty if you have a great result with cardio, but your body will look the same, only smaller. You will still have that pot belly, just a smaller version; and your arms will still look soft. You just end up as a smaller version of a body shape you were already unhappy with.

Perhaps one of the biggest dangers of cardio is that many people justify eating more because they have had a long workout. In addition to eating more, they often unknowingly eat the wrong things, including processed foods, including fruit juices, which are high in sugar. But what's worse is when people finish a workout and go straight to the snacks they really know they shouldn't be eating, justifying it by telling themselves they had a long workout. If it takes five minutes to eat the amount of calories it took you an hour to burn, then what's the point?

One woman who e-mailed me said she was doing *seven hours of cardio per week* and still wasn't getting the results she wanted. She even asked me if she should do more! Marathon runners or triathletes often do even more cardio than that and still struggle with body fat, so obviously cardio is not the best fat burning solution. Don't expect to get maximum fat loss results doing only cardio, even if you're doing more than five hours per week. Obviously, the answer isn't to do more long, slow cardio; the answer is to use interval training – alternating periods of high and low intensity exercise. Interval training is similar to cardio, but gives you more results in less time. But old habits are hard to break, and many people just have the mindset that more is better. In reality, interval training is the better way to get results from your fat burning program.

Interval Training vs. Cardio

Research shows that interval training—short bursts of harder than normal exercise followed by slow recovery—is actually better for fat burning and losing belly fat than long, slow cardio. Back in the mid-1990s, a Canadian research study compared high intensity interval training, also known as H.I.I.T, against a long, slow cardio program. This was a twelve- to fifteen-week program using young men and women and found that the short burst, high intensity interval training resulted in more body fat loss than the longer cardio sessions.

If you still feel you just have to do long cardio, then running is the most productive, though this is not without its caveats. It's rare to find a runner who hasn't spent a lot of time in the doctor's office for lower back, knee, hip, or ankle problems. This is because they do so much volume and of the same movement, which wears on the exact same joints in the exact same way. So as I mentioned before, if you're not going to give cardio up, at least do different types of training.

If you still don't believe me when I say that cardio is a waste of time, take a look at this research. In one study, a large group of men and women did an hour of cardio six days per week for an entire year. The average weight loss after that entire year was just over six pounds for men and women combined. That's three hundred hours of exercise for six pounds of weight loss! That's not a very efficient use of anyone's time.

When I begin Turbulence Training with people, however, depending on how overweight they are, I expect to easily see at least one pound of weight loss per week. In about two months there should be about eight pounds of weight loss. Compared to the study above, Turbulence Training is the obvious answer.

Someone who's overweight and not active could actually see five to seven pounds of weight loss in the first week of Turbulence Training.

When you have less weight to lose, it's harder to do that—so a woman who's 110 pounds shouldn't expect to lose five to seven pounds in the first week, let alone the first month. Still, in one of the Turbulence Training programs being used on MensHealth.com, it's not uncommon for guys to lose more than fifteen pounds in only eight weeks. I'm hearing results of twenty pounds on average and even up to forty-one pounds of fat loss after about eight weeks. These guys are even amazing me with the results.

The Cardio Appetite Connection

It's not that cardio doesn't work at all, ever. In one particular study, one subject lost about thirty pounds in eight weeks. In fact, the average weight loss was eight to twelve pounds. But there was a dark side to cardio in this study, as some subjects actually gained an average of three and a half pounds while on the cardio program. What researchers found when they looked at these subjects' diets is that they consumed an extra three hundred calories per day. These subjects are called *compensators*. This means that people—at least some people—will compensate for their cardio exercise by eating more calories and therefore either wiping out all of the results from the training or even making things worse.

I don't want to sound the alarm that people actually gain fat directly from cardio because I haven't seen that, but overeating, as "compensation" for doing cardio, is a potential problem. Although you can find studies that talk about the benefits of long cardio, they rarely mention the downsides such as overuse injuries or overeating.

By contrast, in an Australian study, researchers found that interval training done on a stationary bicycle helped women lose more belly fat than another group of women doing a slow, long cardio training program. Each group trained about three days per week, and the women on the short burst interval training lost much more belly fat than the women doing the long workouts. The important thing about this study in relation to appetite control is that the interval training—a component of my short burst exercise system—increased hormones in the body called *catecholamines*, which are generally associated with a decrease in appetite and an increase in fat burning.

The interval training group did eight seconds of hard work followed by twelve seconds of recovery repeated for twenty minutes on a special exercise bike. The other group used slow cardio for forty minutes. The cardio training group didn't lose any weight at all over the entire fifteen-week program, yet the interval training group lost several pounds of belly fat. When compared side to side, you should see that all cardio has to offer is time and repetition, while interval training is a key component of Turbulence Training's multifaceted attack designed to target belly fat.

Beating Belly Fat

The three components to the best belly fat program are as follows:

- √ **Nutrition.** You cannot out train a bad diet, so you have to make sure that you're eating fewer calories than you need and preferably with all natural foods.

- √ **Strength training.** You need to put intense resistance on your muscles in order to boost your metabolism.

- √ **Interval training.** Short burst interval training sessions help you burn more belly fat in less time.

In my Turbulence Training workout programs, each training program comes with a four-week interval training system. It will show you how to do a warm-up, how long to do each interval, and instructions on how to do the recovery interval between each set. You can get these at TurbulenceTraining.com/freegift, where we can also help you plan out the best interval training program possible to avoid overuse injuries but also allow you to get maximum results in minimum time. The Turbulence Training interval workout programs will show you how to do get the most out of your workout whether you're outside running on a track or inside on an elliptical machine.

Chapter Three
Short Burst Exercise:
The Belly Fat Solution

Most people think that they can reduce their belly fat by doing endless amounts of abdominal crunches and sit-ups. But it's just not possible. There are other, better ways that you can lose belly fat, such as boosting your metabolism and using the short burst exercise system. The most important thing you need to do to get rid of your belly fat is to use interval training. A research study from Australia shows that women on an interval training program were actually able to lose more belly fat than from any other part of their body while women using the longer cardio program didn't lose belly fat. In addition, I've used Turbulence Training with the most popular fitness magazine in the world on their Web site, menshealth.com, as their belly off program for 2008. In this program, that's where we're seeing the guys losing fifteen to twenty pounds and often even more—including one guy who lost forty-one pounds in eight weeks using the belly off program, which is built around the short burst exercise system of strength training, bodyweight training, and interval training.

It's important to keep in mind that there are different kinds of belly fat. If you have ever seen guys with very hard, round bellies that stick straight out, that is generally referred to as visceral fat. Visceral fat is around the organs and underneath the muscles of the abdominal wall and is particularly unhealthy, as opposed to someone whose belly is just soft and hangs over. That's subcutaneous fat, which means it's fat underneath the skin but over top of the abdominal wall. Subcutaneous fat is the same type of fat that you see under your chin and love handles. While it's not very healthy either, it's not as dangerous as visceral fat.

Short burst exercise can be both strength training using bodyweight exercises and dumbbell and barbell exercises, or it can be interval training. When you're doing short burst exercise with resistance, I prefer that you use eight repetitions per set rather than fifteen repetitions per set like most trainers recommend in fat loss programs. When you do interval training, you're going hard for a short amount of time and then going down to a very slow, easily paced recovery for generally two to three times as long as the hard interval duration. Most importantly, people have to understand that it's going to take more mental effort to do those short burst exercise sessions, but in two ways it's going to result in a shorter workout. First, your workout is going to seem like it goes by faster. Even if you only do twenty minutes of cardio, twenty steady-state minutes are going to seem like a much longer period of time than twenty minutes of interval training. Most people find steady-state cardio boring. But when you do twenty minutes of interval training, the work interval may seem like a long time but the recovery interval is going to go by very quickly. By adjusting those levels of intensity, it makes for a much more enjoyable session overall, and you're going to get more results in much less time.

In my Turbulence Training programs, I prefer people to train only three days per week, which means only three structured workouts per week that include both strength and interval training within the same workout. That gets you done in less than forty-five minutes. A lot of people have to adjust mentally for that, especially if they're coming from doing ninety minute workouts, five or six days per week, with the long, slow, lower intensity cardio sessions. With Turbulence Training, you're simply just substituting quality, high intensity work for time. I prefer three workouts per week, but for those who are very busy and only have twenty minutes to work out each session, you can do six workouts per week: strength training on one day, interval training the next, and just alternate for those six days. I haven't found any difference in which one is better, but whatever fits your lifestyle is most important. It all comes down to consistency.

Contrast Between Old, Ineffective Fat Loss Programs & Turbulence Training

	Old Ineffective Fat Loss Program	Turbulence Training 3d/week	Turbulence Training 6d/week
Monday	90 minutes weights plus cardio	45 minutes Strength & Intervals	20 min Strength
Tuesday	90 minutes weights plus cardio	30 minutes fun activity (dog walk, sports, etc.)	20 min Intervals
Wednesday	90 minutes weights plus cardio	45 minutes Strength & Intervals	20 min Strength
Thursday	90 minutes weights plus cardio	30 minutes fun activity (dog walk, sports, etc.)	20 min Intervals
Friday	90 minutes weights plus cardio	45 minutes Strength & Intervals	20 min Strength
Saturday	45 minutes cardio plus abs	30 minutes fun activity (dog walk, sports, etc.)	20 min Intervals
Sunday	45 minutes cardio plus abs	30 minute walk with family	30 minute walk with family

Benefits for Women

Many women are scared that any sort of strength training means bulking up. But bulking up is a matter of eating more food than you need, so if you aren't honest with how many calories you're consuming in a day and you overeat, you will continue to gain weight. We have quite a few success stories on TurbulenceTraining.com of women who have obviously not bulked up by using strength training. They have done just the opposite in fact. We have women weighing as little as 110 pounds who did not gain any weight by using the Turbulence Training system, and we have lots of women who have lost a lot of body fat, tightened up their bodies, and toned their muscles because of the strength training component. They simply got the metabolism boost of the strength training and maintained their muscle mass. Even if they did gain a little bit of muscle mass, it doesn't show up as being big and bulky because our Turbulence Training system uses bodyweight and total body workouts, neither of which are going to create an overly muscular female bodybuilder physique. If you are very concerned about it, simply substitute more bodyweight exercises for dumbbell exercises or ask for exercise substitutions on the Turbulence Training website message board. Just as you can customize your workout based on your schedule, you can customize your workout to get around any mental fear of bulking up and still get maximum benefits from that strength training portion of Turbulence Training.

Another benefit of Turbulence Training for women is that strength training results in greater bone density. Most women's programs, if they involve only cardio, will only increase bone density in the legs and a little bit in the spine as well. With more intense strength training that works the entire body, bone density is increased in such vulnerable places as the wrists, arms, and hips.

Interval training works really well for women mostly because they come from a long history of slow, low intensity exercise. When they jump over to higher intensity short burst exercise, their bodies respond to it. Their bodies had adapted to the easy cardio that was never hard enough to get results in the first place, and when they finally make that switch over to higher intensity interval training, they get all the results they never did before.

Women are often the greatest success stories because they're just not used to this type of training. Too many magazines had shown them too many times that cardio is the only way to do things, or maybe their trainers had never respected their physical ability in the past. Whatever the reason, many women have never bothered to push their bodies as hard as they should, and because of it these same women had never gotten results. By respecting the strength and fitness capacities of women, this new stimulus just ends up helping them break through a plateau in performance and burn body fat at the same time.

One of my best female success stories is a woman named Kristine Willis, who started out at 183 pounds and decreased to 167 pounds in our twelve-week transformation contest while losing 4 inches from her waist and 2 inches from her hips. The great thing about Kristine is that she looks ten years younger, and the fact is she looked ten years younger within the first four weeks of the program. She loves the training; she finds it fun, and she's getting the results that she's always wanted. And with a work schedule as busy as hers, by working out less, her lifestyle has benefited because she now has more time to do the things she wants.

The Mistake Men Make

When I started out strength training, I made the same mistake that many men do, training like Arnold Schwarzenegger. That meant six days a week with heavy weights. And like so many guys do, I ended up with some overuse injuries. It's the same side effect as running too much, which I discuss in the "Dark Side of Cardio." If you're training like Arnold did, six days per week, your shoulder is eventually going to end up with some type of problem because there's almost no way to avoid stressing the shoulder joint when strength training, especially if you do a lot of bench pressing and shoulder presses. That's why Turbulence Training gives you a day off in between total body strength training workouts so that your joints and muscles can recover.

With short burst workouts, you increase the amount of fat burning hormones called catecholamines. These hormones are also known as adrenaline. They've been shown to help decrease appetite and increase calorie burning after exercise. The short burst exercise system is perfect for guys who don't want the skinny, weak physique that comes from running sixty to ninety minutes on a treadmill, not to mention the injuries associated with it. Short bursts workouts are similar to the type of training you did as a young athlete, and your body recognizes and responds to that more than with low intensity workouts.

My best male success story is a great young guy named Juan Ruiz from Michigan. He started Turbulence Training at over three hundred pounds, and in nine months has lost over one hundred pounds! He has lost almost his entire beer belly because he's done exactly what the program recommends. He's one of those guys who went from doing absolutely nothing but sitting on the couch to using the beginner Turbulence Training program. That's why he was able to lose such a great amount of weight. He was really happy once he got under 240, ecstatic when he got under 230; and when he finally got down to 220, it was the first time he had weighed so little in his adult life.

At the same time, I've had busy dads get their six-pack abs back. Mark Russo and Andy Apsay are regular 30-something guys—and now look like they are one step away from being on the cover of *Men's Health* magazine. There's also Steve Hays from Arizona who lost thirty-three pounds in twelve weeks using the Turbulence Training program and now looks fifteen years younger. Whether it's Steve or Juan or any of my other guys, it just goes to show that Turbulence Training benefits any age or body type. Read about more success stories at TurbulenceTraining.com.

The Short Burst Exercise Transformation Contest

I run three transformation contests per year that each last twelve weeks. The contest requirements are that you have to provide a before and after photo, and you have to use the Turbulence Training work-outs. We allow a time period for people to start, so generally, I announce the contest and give people four weeks to have their official start date. For example, if I start a program or announce the contest on May 1, contestants have until May 31 to submit their *before* photos. We prefer people to log their daily diet and workouts on the transformation forum at TTMembers.com because social support is one of the most overlooked aspects of fat loss.

There is so much support from people around the world that everyone gets more results when they do that. Although it's not a requirement, I highly recommend it. We've seen such incredible changes, whether it's a skinny girl going from a good body to an amazing body, or a forty-five-year old woman who is overweight because she's had kids and just never lost the baby fat. These women are losing up to fifteen pounds in the twelve-week program and looking like they're ten years younger, while on the men's side, guys have actually gained muscle while losing fat in our twelve-week program. Our best result in the twelve-week transformation program, so far, was Steve Hays who lost thirty-three pounds of ugly fat.

The typical results for men are a loss of fifteen pounds of body fat, or six percent body fat. If a guy is at nineteen percent body fat to start, he'll get down to around thirteen percent fat after 12 weeks. Once you're down around that point, you'll start seeing the top two of your abs and will be getting close to the six-pack, which you can generally get around ten percent body fat. Men will typically lose a lot of body fat and even gain a little bit of muscle mass, while the guys who are really overweight will lose inches and inches and really decrease the size of their belly. If there's any bad thing to the transformation contest, it's that you will need a little bit of money to spend on a new wardrobe (but that's okay, because the winner takes home $2000!).

For the girls, the numbers will be a little bit smaller, but we're looking at twelve to fifteen pounds of body fat loss over the course of twelve weeks or about two to four inches from the waist and hips. The contestants really love being able to fit into their old clothes or going out to buy newer, slimmer stuff that now fits. They are also losing— and I had never heard this term until I started the transformation con- test—what they call the *muffin top*, which is the fat that hangs over the top of tight jeans. The first transformation contest winner in 2008, Emily Johnson, has an incredible before and after photo in her favor- ite jeans. She had the muffin top before the twelve-week program, but now she fits into those jeans about as well as anyone could. Check out her photos at TransformationContest.com.

We'll talk about inspiration in Chapter 9, but because of the twelve-week deadline, the spirit of competition, and the prize money, the transformation contest is one of the biggest motivators you could possibly have. By entering the contest and posting it on our forum, you are creating accountability within the Turbulence Training online community. Everybody likes to belong so, by having a contest, this gives people a little exclusive group that they can belong to, a little badge of honor. It brings people together in a way that I don't think a regular forum without a contest could.

The best thing about the contest is that it doesn't matter who you are or what kind of shape you're in. We have both men and women, skinny and overweight; the program has fit all body types and lifestyles. And while this isn't a competition in the sense that you are going against anyone, by keeping up with the other contestants on the Web site, you can really help motivate each other and be supportive.

Here are a couple of essays written to me by two contestants. I hope they give you a more personal view of why people enter and what they can get out of it.

"The TT transformation contest has been an unbelievable journey and an incredible learning experience for me. When I began my transformation, I had been trying for years to lose weight. I was already working out, doing intervals, and eating well much of the time, but I never seemed to make any meaningful progress. I was partially being held back by the destructive cycles that I found myself falling into over and over with food. Intellectually I knew perfectly well what I needed to be eating, but I had had such a difficult and negative relationship with food for so many years that as soon as I would begin eating healthy and making progress I would immediately sabotage myself by binging only to end up back where I started and more frustrated with myself than before.

"The transformation contest finally gave me the accountability and social support that I needed to jump-start permanent change, and TT provided me with the fastest and most effective tool to get where I wanted to be. What I appreciate most about Craig's system is its simplicity. I am now spending less time in the gym than before and getting my best results ever. Of course, although the TT workouts are intense, fun, and incredibly effective, they were only one of several contributing factors to my success.

"Besides the TT workouts themselves, having a clear goals and a plan to achieve them, eating clean food consistently, finding a diet that worked for me (EatStopEat.com), and social support and accountability were the other key factors in making my transformation a success. I never realized how much of a difference social support can really make, but being surrounded by the other amazing people on the TT forum who were all working towards a similar goal and facing similar challenges was an integral part of keeping me motivated and moving towards my goal. The encouragement, advice, knowledge, and inspiration I received from the forum were truly priceless.

"Today I feel healthy and strong, I have completely transformed my relationship with food so that I now find that making good food choices is no longer a struggle. I'm closer than ever to my dream body, and I was able to take "after pictures" fitting comfortably into a pair of size 27 jeans that I haven't fit into in years! And I achieved all of this despite visits from friends, an eleven-day trip to Morocco where I had much less control over my nutrition, and being hit by illness at the end of my challenge. I feel confident that the lessons I have learned about goal achievement, accountability, and social support will carry over into all other areas of my life.

"And with the good habits that I have established over the course of the contest, along with the endless variety of TT workouts, I know that *it will be easy for me to make continued progress. It is hard for me to find adequate words to sum up all the different ways that my life has been positively affected by this contest and the gratitude that I feel. I guess the only thing I can say is thanks so much to Craig for creating this incredible system and to all of my fellow transformers who were an unending source of motivation, support, and inspiration."*

Emily Johnson

"I've been putting off submitting my essay because it's difficult to find the words to express the difference the TT program has made in my life. I don't feel like the same person I was on January 1st. So many times in the past, the beginning of a new year came and I vowed to make changes in my life. My problem was that I didn't know what changes to make. In previous years I didn't have the courage or motivation to actually follow through with my dream of reaching my goal weight; I always made excuses.

"With Turbulence Training I didn't have anything to lose but weight! You'd never guess from my before photos but I was actually spending more time at the gym before I started TT. I would often go to the gym and spend twenty minutes on the bike, twenty minutes on the treadmill, and then twenty minutes on the elliptical, all in an effort to lose fat. I can't believe how much time I wasted! The fact that Turbulence Training only takes forty-five minutes for a workout was definitely something that piqued my interest from the very beginning. The intervals are so much more effective, and I'm gaining muscle.

"Here are my stats from the beginning and the end of my transformation. (Sorry, but I don't know what my body fat measurements were before or after.)

My starting measurements:
weight: 183 lbs.
chest: 43"
waist: 38"
hips: 44"
My final measurements:
weight: 167 lbs. (-16 lbs.)
chest: 41" (-2")
waist: 34" (-4")
hips: 41 ¾" (-2 ¼")

"I logged my food intake in FitDay.com, which helped me see if I was eating a well-balanced diet. It was interesting to see if I was getting all of the nutrients my body needed, and it helped me find balance on the days I had a few extra treats. I loved being able to read about everyone else's journey as well. The support network at TTmembers.com is incredible. The words of encouragement, the suggestions, and the support that was always available helped keep me accountable but also helped keep me strong. I realized I was not alone in my journey.
"By learning an effective, efficient way to work out and having support along my journey I've begun to make changes in my appearance that have helped me my find my inner strength and confidence. Thanks to participating in the TT Transformation Contest I'm ready to take on new challenges and I'm no longer making excuses for not following my dreams."

Kristine Willis

"I have been an obese male all of my life. In August of 2007 I weighed in at 315 pounds, the most I have ever weighed. I have tried many diets and exercise plans, but nothing has really worked well for

me. I was at the end of my rope and really starting to look into bariatric surgery. Even though it has worked wonders for my friends and family, though, I never wanted that surgery for myself. To have that surgery would mean that I would never know how good it felt to lose weight on my own, to find the discipline and mental fortitude to push myself and watch what I am eating. How long would it be before I gained back that lost weight after the surgery because I never learned how to really be healthy?

"In early August I found Turbulence Training, and signed up for the FREE Report—The Dark Side of Cardio. I have to admit, it piqued my interest. I was so disgusted with what I read because it was so true. I couldn't tell you how many hours I have wasted doing just cardio and staying away from weights, only to watch my body stay the exact same. I knew that I needed to get Turbulence Training. I knew that TT was going to change my life forever. I wasn't wrong.

"I also knew though that any workout program I used wouldn't be successful if I didn't change my eating habits. I started a low carb regimen, eating only complex carbs and allowing myself a cheat meal once a month. I started TT in August 2007, since then I have lost a total of 86 pounds (it is now March 3, 2008). I have never looked better in my life, and I have never felt better in my life. For the first time in my life I have signed up for a fitness contest. Never did anyone, let alone myself, think that I of all people would be signing up for a fitness contest!

Yet here I am. I have gone through eighty-four days of this contest. During the contest I have had quite a few challenges—a month-long plateau, final exams, and a bum shoulder, just to name a few; but I have also met some of the greatest people through this contest, people who are trying to do the same thing I am doing—live a healthier lifestyle. They have been some of the most understanding, caring, and motivational people I could have ever had the pleasure to meet.

"I started this contest using the Original TT workout. After that I went into the TT 2K3 workout program, and finished this contest with the four-week Intermediate Bodyweight program. In this contest I have had gains and losses; I have learned the benefits of fasting and how to fast properly. I have learned how to truly eat balanced meals and how to keep pushing myself when I have nothing else left to give. I have also learned how to cope with injuries and how to not let them get the best of me. I have been able to do most of this mainly because of the great people involved in this fitness contest. Their inspiring words have kept me honest with myself and have helped me keep my head up when I just wanted to hang it down in defeat. I have learned that you may lose a battle here and there, but the war is far from over.

"I have lost three inches from my chest, four from my gut, three from my waist, ¾ inches from my biceps, ¼ of an inch from my thighs, and twenty-five pounds since starting this twelve-week transformation contest. I am far from being done, and even when I finally hit my goal weight, my journey will not end there. My journey will last me a lifetime; every day will be another day to strive for a healthier, more active me.

"When I think about living this way for a lifetime, it doesn't overwhelm me. I am grateful that my obesity didn't cripple my body, that I still have a chance to reverse the side effects, and that I am healthy enough to go to the gym and use my body to its full potential. Granted, to win a prize in this contest would be sweet, but whether I win a prize or not, it doesn't matter. I already feel like a winner. Throughout this contest I have learned so many valuable lessons, and I have met some of the most motivational people anyone could meet. I am a lot healthier today than I was when I started this contest, I have joined my first fitness contest ever, and I have stuck with it through the end."

Juan Ruiz

Chapter Four
The Ultimate Home Gym

I've found that many women like to avoid commercial gyms because they find them very intimidating. Some women have problems with guys staring at them or are intimidated by the young cardio bunnies. Even guys can find some commercial gyms intimidating depending on the people that go there, or that members are discourteous and don't wipe down equipment after using it. The music is a point of contention for some, and a lot of people just don't like the gym "scene."

Personally, I really like the commercial gyms, and I wouldn't discourage anyone from using them. But if you can work out at home, you can obviously save quite a bit of money, because even a cheap commercial gym membership, at least in the city of Toronto where I live, is forty dollars per month. You can buy an exercise bench, dumbbell set, and exercise ball from a used sporting goods store for under $150 total. Jumping rope is great for interval training, and it requires a very small amount of space; you can do it in your garage. So, it's much more economical to stay at home. Plus you save time and gas not having to drive to and from the gym.

At home, you don't end up having conversations at the gym that waste your time. You really can get more done in less time at home, and you can work out whenever you want—early in the morning before the gym opens, late at night, or even on holidays. There's nothing magical about the gym; it's really about your attitude, your intensity, and the program that you're following.

Most people can get by with a very small ten-by-ten space in their basement because they're just doing exercises on the bench, the exercise ball, or while lying down on the floor for push-ups. Storing your equipment won't require a lot of space; we're not talking about one of those huge multi-exercise gyms in your basement that people used to have back in the 1980s. Since many of the Turbulence Training exercises are bodyweight only, you can even exercise in your hotel room when you're on the road or outside if the weather is nice.

To do all of the Turbulence Training exercises, you'll need an exercise ball, exercise bench, and a set of adjustable dumbbells (a pull-up bar is a bonus if you are strong enough for that exercise). Your bodyweight and the exercise ball allow you to do dozens of fat burning exercises. The dumbbells are very important for people who need extra resistance to add weight to the workouts, while the pull-up bar is just the icing on the cake, because it allows you to do pull-ups, chin-ups, and bodyweight rows. However, you can do ninety percent of the exercises without it. Each Turbulence Training exercise or program has alternative dumbbell exercises for people that don't have pull-up bars. It's tough to train your upper back, but as long as you have either dumbbells or the pull-up bar, you can train those muscles and get maximum results.

I have bought cheap used dumbbells at Play It Again Sports, and you can get inexpensive exercise balls at Wal-Mart. As long as it rolls properly, that's the most important thing.

The Commercial Gym Myth

A lot of magazines and trainers will tell you that you need to do cardio on fancy machines or that you need to come in and use their weight machines. Of course they tell you this because they spent a lot of money on their machines—but these machines simply aren't best way to lose weight. It doesn't matter how much they spent on their equipment. That stuff isn't necessary to get maximum results.

You can lose body fat doing any type of exercise and any type of work. You can get a great body by using only your body weight. The one "machine" that I do like to use is the seated cable row. It takes up a lot of space to have at home, however, so you probably won't have one; but if you do train at the gym it helps you train your back. As I said, it's very difficult to train your back without having dumbbells or the seated row machine or the pull-up bar.

Another downfall of the machines is the calorie counting feature. A CBS News Report actually took a look at the calorie counting on certain cardio machines and found that they overestimated in almost all situations. So those who go to the gym and won't leave until they've burned three hundred calories on a machine are really being deceived. More importantly it's not the amount of calories you burn in a workout that guarantees fat loss, but the way you train. To base your standard for exercising on how many calories the machine says you've burned is just asking for a letdown. Instead, I encourage you to focus on the *quality* of exercise. When you do that, the machines and the calorie counters just don't matter anymore.

Part of the challenge of Turbulence Training is having to un-learn a lot of what you know about fitness; some people just cannot shake the idea of not doing long, slow cardio. They may enjoy it, dark side and all, so if you find yourself wanting to do cardio at home, the machine I recommend is the stationary cycle. It allows you to do hard workouts but without worrying about falling off or ending up with a hamstring injury from running too fast. Treadmills give you great results, and you can either do walking or running on it, but you need to be very careful when doing intervals. I have to put the elliptical machine in third place. Some people report better results than others, but those are three cardio machines that don't take up a huge amount of space. Just make sure that you get something that is high quality and built to last.

If you don't have any machines you can still do interval-like training with just bodyweight exercises. For example, you could do thirty seconds of bodyweight squats followed by sixty seconds of recovery. However for even better results, I recommend bodyweight circuits in which you alternate between upper and lower body exercises. Do six to eight bodyweight exercises in a circuit with no rest between each exercise, and then rest a minute after the circuit before repeating it two to three times.

Another way of doing interval-like training is to use a kettlebell. You can do kettlebell swings for thirty seconds followed by a sixty second rest period in place of conventional interval training. So there are all types of non-traditional interval training methods that don't require you to use a cardio machine and that you can do at home with a little imagination. Whatever you decide to use, always put safety first. As I've said before, it's hard to get a good workout when you are injured.

To try the Turbulence Training workouts and share your results on the TT Member's forum, visit TurbulenceTraining.com/freegift to get your one month FREE Turbulence Training membership. In the transformation forum or workout journal forum, you can post before and after photos and share with everyone the results of your training.

Chapter Five
The Turbulence Training Workout

Unlike most workouts, Turbulence Training doesn't have you start with a five minute treadmill cardio warm-up and five minutes of stretching. When using a treadmill to warm-up, your muscles and joints are not prepared for a total body strength training workout. While other experts also recommend using the treadmill to increase your core temperature before you work out, this has absolutely no impact on your performance or risk of injury. The most important thing to do is to make sure that your warm up includes specific movements that address each of the individual joints that you're going to exercise. In the case of Turbulence Training, all the workouts are total body workouts, so you have to warm-up the shoulder, elbow, knee, and hip joints—and you can't do that on a treadmill!

A Turbulence Training warm-up includes a lot of my unique bodyweight exercises; they're traditional ones such as the bodyweight squat with some type of twist. For example, in a prisoner squat you put your hands behind your head with your elbows up to the side like a prisoner getting arrested. Then, by bringing your shoulder blades together at the back, you're able to warm-up your upper back. It also adds a little bit of stretch to the chest. By doing this little variation while you're squatting, you warm-up more of the entire body with one simple movement.

Another bodyweight exercise to include in the warm-up is some type of push-up. I like to use variations such as the elevated push-up:

this is done in the regular push-up position but with one hand elevated four to six inches on a block. Doing ten repetitions – five repetitions for one side and five for the other – warms up additional muscles in your torso around your abdominals. It also helps improve shoulder blade movement, since a lot of people have shoulder mobility problems. With this push-up variation, you're increasing the movement of the scapula and the shoulder joint and helping to eliminate some of the problems that come from sitting at a desk all day. If you are a beginner, you can do the push-ups on your knees.

Those are just two of the bodyweight movements that belong in a warm-up. When I do the bodyweight circuits to warm-up, I like to make sure that the front of the torso, the upper back, the abdominals, and the lower body are all warmed up. So I like to add exercise ball leg curls to warm-up the lower body, a "stick-up" exercise to warm-up the upper back, and an exercise like mountain climbers to warm-up the abdominals.

I recommend that you go through the bodyweight warm-up circuit two times using the examples I just mentioned: prisoner squats, elevated push-ups, exercise ball leg curls, stick-ups, and mountain climbers. Do ten repetitions of the first exercise, then without rest go immediately to the next exercise, and so on. Once you've gone through that circuit once, rest one minute before repeating that circuit one more time. This should take about three to five minutes, after which you are well prepared to move on into any specific warm-up exercises. In other words, if you're doing dumbbell chest presses, you'll still need to do a specific warm up set for that exercise. By warming up with bodyweight exercises your body is much more prepared for a total body strength training and interval training than by walking on a treadmill. And of course, the warm-up has to be adjusted for the fitness level of the individual. A full body warm-up for someone who's been sitting on the couch for a few years is going to be much lighter than that of a professional athlete. But while the exercises or duration might be different, the principles are the same.

Turbulence Training Workout Set-up

Bodyweight Circuit	5 Minutes
Strength Training Supersets	15-20 Minutes
Interval Training	15-20 Minutes
Stretching	5 Minutes

Bodybuilding versus Strength Training

The reason you shouldn't train like a bodybuilder is that if you're like most people, you will end up injured from spending five or six days per week on strength training alone and you don't have that much time to commit to it anyway. In fact, the next time you're at the gym, ask a bodybuilder what sort of injuries he has; you're almost guaranteed to hear a long list of joint problems starting with the shoulder. When lifting heavy weights as often as most bodybuilders do, even a small mistake in form can result in injury. The beauty of Turbulence Training is that the exercises are always changing, and we're never putting more stress on the joints then they can handle.

One way I avoid overuse injury is by using total body multi-muscle exercises. Squats are a great example of a multi-muscle exercise. This could be anything from a barbell squat to a dumbbell squat to a bodyweight squat or even a split squat. You're using that squatting motion—in which you drop your hips, push them back, bend your knees, go down to parallel keeping your back flat, and then push through all those muscles to come back up. That's one of the best exercises for maximizing the amount of muscle you work in the shortest amount of time.

Turbulence Training also uses supersets, in which you take two strength training exercises and do them back-to-back with little or no rest, to get more results in less time. In traditional bodybuilding workouts, you'll see guys do supersets of dumbbell chest presses followed by dumbbell chest flies, or maybe leg presses followed by leg extensions. That's an effective superset for building muscle, but that's not the type of superset we use in the Turbulence Training workouts.

In Turbulence Training, we use non-competing supersets, meaning that the two exercises use two different groups of muscles. This might be a lower body exercise and an upper body exercise, such as a squat paired with a chin-up. I also like pairing a pushing exercise and a pulling exercise in a superset, such as a dumbbell chest press and a dumbbell row, so that the chest muscles rest while the rowing muscles work and vice versa. Usually, I make sure the hardest exercise is the first exercise in the superset.

One thing to be careful of in non-competing supersets, especially if you're doing a lot of dumbbell work, is to make sure that you don't have exercises competing for grip strength. That would occur if you did a dumbbell split squat, which is a traditional exercise in Turbulence Training, along with a dumbbell row, because you're holding the dumbbells with your grip strength in both exercises.

One of the Turbulence Training workouts, The Dumbbell Bodyweight Fusion Workout is specifically designed to avoid grip strength fatigue, by pairing a dumbbell exercise with a bodyweight exercise in all supersets. For example, you could do a dumbbell chest press paired with a chin-up or a dumbbell row paired with a decline push-up. For the lower body, you could have a dumbbell split squat paired with an exercise ball leg curl. Another good solution for avoiding grip strength fatigue is to use a barbell that can be rested across the back for exercises like squats and lunges.

Interval Training to Burn Belly Fat

As I mentioned before, when you're doing interval training, it's very important to warm-up specifically for the type of exercise you're going to do ahead. This should be obvious, and something that you do naturally. For example, if you're going to do intervals on the bike, warm-up on the bike. Start off at a very easy pace, and over the five-minute warm up gradually increase the intensity until you build up to your regular cardio pace. Then take the intensity down for a minute before doing your first hard interval bout.

For those at the advanced fitness level who are running sprints as your interval training, make sure you warm-up for additional time. The high velocity and increased range of motion that occurs during sprinting can lead to injuries, which is why I prefer stationary cycling as the simplest, most effective, and safest method of doing interval training.

There's actually no "best" interval duration, according to the research studies. Some fitness experts recommend that people do twenty seconds of hard work followed by ten seconds of recovery repeated eight times for a total of four minutes, while others, like myself, think that a nice, simple thirty-second interval followed by sixty to ninety seconds of recovery is very effective for fat loss. In the research study from Australia that helped prove the effectiveness of interval training, they had their subjects do eight seconds of intervals followed by twelve seconds of recovery, and that was repeated over and over again for twenty minutes. That is difficult to replicate in the gym on most pieces of cardio equipment, because most of them take ten to fifteen seconds just to change the intensity to the correct level. In fact, the subjects in the Australian study were using a specific bike not readily available in gyms, but you can follow the same workout with running or biking outside. But, as I mentioned earlier, you must take extra precautions if you choose to use running for interval training.

For beginners, I like to use longer intervals, having them exercise slightly harder than a normal cardio pace for one minute followed by exercise at a recovery pace for two minutes. That's a great starting place for beginners, and eventually they progress to the advanced interval program of thirty-second intervals of hard exercise done at an eight or nine out of ten intensity level followed by sixty to ninety seconds of recovery.

There's an endless number of ways that you can do interval training. As I mentioned before, I prefer the bike for simplicity and safety. Obviously, running outside is very, very effective, the most effective form of interval training is likely sprinting around a track or uphill— but again, that can place you at a higher risk for injury. Running on a treadmill is fine, as are the elliptical and rowing machines, although I personally haven't had clients have the greatest success with elliptical machines. I find that they can fool you into using a lower level of intensity than you really should be using—but I have known people to use every type of machine in the gym and get results as long as they use interval training. You can swim, cycle outside, walk or run up hills. And then some of the lesser-known ways to do interval training are strongman events such as tire flipping, farmer walks, or kettlebell training—swings and snatches.

For people that don't have any cardio equipment at home or kettlebells or tires to flip around, bodyweight circuits are the best alternative. I set up interval training with bodyweight circuits as follows: choose three lower body exercises and three upper body exercises and alternate between the two. For example, you could do a squat followed by a push-up. Those would be your introductory exercises, and then you could increase the intensity by going to a lunge and a bodyweight row. Then finish up with a step up and a mountain climber, which is an upper body exercise that also targets the abs. Do each of those exercises for ten to fifteen repetitions, without resting between exercises. At the end of the circuit, rest one minute, and repeat the circuit two to three more times. That will get you a bodyweight circuit workout done in about twenty minutes. To see an example of bodyweight circuit training video, go to Youtube and search for Turbulence Training or Craig Ballantyne.

Each Turbulence Training workout ends with stretching. It's very important to stretch tight muscle groups—that is, muscle groups that are very inflexible, rather than focusing on muscles that are already very flexible. For example, if someone has flexible hamstrings, there's not a whole lot of extra benefit for them to stretch those hamstrings if their quadriceps are tight. If they do, this could actually lead to injury.

Most people, because of their desk jockey jobs, end up with a lot of very tight muscles, and with rounded shoulder posture and will benefit from stretching and opening up the chest. Doing that can also help avoid any shoulder injuries, because the tightness there can actually end up affecting the way you do certain exercises. If you follow the Turbulence Training stretching program, you'll do six to eight stretches at the end of your workout. They help with the tightest parts of the body, and all you have to do is hold each position for thirty seconds with some tension but not to the point of discomfort. If you do need additional flexibility work, you can do each stretch two or three times, and you can also do them over the course of the day, even when you're not exercising.

To try the Turbulence Training for fat loss workouts, visit TurbulenceTraining.com/freegift to get your one month FREE Turbulence Training membership. These workouts will show you exactly how to get maximum results in minimum time and you'll be able to see exercise photos, descriptions, and videos for all of the exercises and stretches. The Turbulence Training program takes you through your fat burning workouts step-by-step. There's also a workout chart to record your weights and the repetitions done so you can constantly refer back and make sure that you're improving over time.

Chapter Six
The Secrets to Great Bodyweight Workouts

Bodyweight exercises are the perfect combination of strength training and interval training. They're not really a hard-core strength training exercise, but some like chin-ups or one-leg squats can be pretty tough. Most bodyweight exercises can be done for quite a few repetitions, so they take on a bit of an interval training effect. This allows you to get the best of both worlds and burn body fat, maintain muscle mass, and boost your metabolism. Bodyweight exercises are the perfect fit in a short-burst exercise system based on multi-muscle exercises, and you can get a lot of results in very little time.

It might not seem like you can burn fat just by using your bodyweight, but you can. Multi-muscle bodyweight abdominal exercises can also help you get the washboard abs that you want. I don't use sit-ups and crunches in my programs, but you can do mountain climbers, exercise ball jackknives, hanging knee-ups, and hanging leg raises to sculpt your abs. They are fun, and sure are a lot more interesting than doing hundreds of stomach crunches, and more effective, too. You can get more home abdominal workouts at TurbulenceTrainingForAbs.com.

Push-ups also work your abs, and there are twenty or thirty different ways you can do push-ups alone by varying hand position, elevating your feet, elevating one of your hands, and incorporating your lower body into the movement. The Spiderman push-up is a very unique exercise; you lower your body to the floor while bringing your knee up to your elbow. Because you're only on one leg it increases the amount of abdominal work that you're doing. You can also do bodyweight exercises such as pull-ups, chin-ups, and inverted rows for your back. In the inverted row, you lie underneath a bar set at hip height, and then row your chest up to the bar. It's an excellent exercise for the upper back. You can also do an exercise called the pike push-up or shoulder press push-up, which works your shoulders a lot more than regular push-ups. This involves putting your feet up on a bench, piking your hips up in the air, and trying to be as vertical as possible while doing a push-up that looks like an upside-down shoulder press. As you can see, there are many different types of bodyweight exercises that you can do for your upper body that aren't just the plain old push-up.

Beginners and overweight individuals should start with ab exercises called the plank and the side plank. These are exercises that involve holding your body in one position for a period of time. This helps build abdominal endurance, which I'll talk about later, and it's really important for keeping your lower back healthy. I also use the exercise ball for a lot of abdominal exercises including an exercise ball jackknife—your elbows are on a bench and your feet are on a ball while you tuck your knees up to your chest, or you can have your hands on the floor in a push-up position and do that same exercise. I also like to use hanging knee raises or hanging leg raises as an advanced abdominal exercise.

I encourage you to avoid sit-ups and even basic crunches and just use these multi-muscle total body abdominal exercises instead. This includes mountain climbers and Spiderman climber exercises, which are done in push-up position and involve bringing your knee up to your chest or your foot up outside your body to your hand.

For the lower body, lunges are the most overused and overrated leg exercise for beginners, because most people can't do them properly. Instead of starting with lunges, beginners should start on the ground with the lying hip extension and lying single-leg hip extension, then move up to bodyweight squat, and then progress to a split squat, which is a static lunge. In the split squat, rather than stepping forward and back with each repetition, you simply step forward and maintain that position while dropping the hips down and up in place. You can use a wall or some other type of support for balance. Once you move up to doing the forward lunge, you can also do diagonal lunges and reverse lunges and finally the one-leg squat and pistol squat. You can see all of these unique abdominal, push-up, and lower body exercises on Youtube by searching Craig Ballantyne or Turbulence Training.

Bodyweight Circuits to Burn Belly Fat

Bodyweight circuits are done in a similar fashion as interval training in that you're going to work hard for a short amount of time and then take a rest, recover, and repeat. Bodyweight circuits might be the best form of exercise available, because you train for strength, fat loss, cardiovascular fitness all at once, going through a wide variety of movements, using a lot of muscle mass, and putting your body into turbulence to burn more calories after training. Alternating between upper and lower body exercises, along with the short recovery after each circuit are necessary so that you can train hard in each circuit.

It's important to make sure that you start your circuit with easy exercises and increase the difficulty as the circuit goes on. In each bodyweight circuit I create, you'll train all the major muscle groups and do a variety of different movement patterns and that way you'll help to avoid any muscle imbalances.

You can use anywhere from six to ten bodyweight exercises for a circuit, so start with something simple like a prisoner or bodyweight squat, then some type of basic push-up, followed by a single-leg exercise and an upper body pulling exercise. From there you can move to another lower body exercise followed by another type of push-up and then finish the circuit with a total body exercise like jumping jacks. Do ten to fifteen repetitions of each exercise, with no rest between each, so by the end of the circuit you will be approaching fatigue. Then rest one minute and go through that two to three more times, for about twenty minutes total. Bodyweight circuit training is not true interval training, but the results are similar.

Bodyweight Circuit Workout Set-up

Easy Lower Body Exercise	Prisoner Squat
Easy Upper Body Exercise	Push-up Variation
Single-Leg Exercise	Split Squat
Hard Upper Body Exercise	Inverted Row
Single-Leg Exercise	Step-ups
Hard Upper Body Exercise	Close-grip Push-ups
Total Body Exercise	Jumping Jacks

So if you do not have cardio equipment at home, or the ability to do interval training outside, simply replace the interval training portion of the workout with bodyweight circuit training. The bodyweight circuit training would be completed after the strength training supersets.

For advanced fat loss results, I sometimes have clients do extra bodyweight circuits on non-Turbulence Training days. But I only let people do this for 2-3 weeks, before having them take a week off from these extra circuits. However, I always choose exercises that will not cause muscle soreness the day after. I try to include one abdominal exercise in each circuit, always choosing a multi-muscle, total body ab exercise, because there's a lot more benefit to them than just lying down on the ground and doing a crunch. Doing hundreds of crunches only trains one muscle group, and can cause repetitive stress injuries, like repetitive cardio. Mountain climbers and exercise ball jackknives, on the other hand, make you use more muscles to stabilize yourself for endurance. You're also using your legs, while at the same time training your abdominals to help you get six-pack abs. Overall, total body ab exercises give you more results in less time.

In some workouts, such as Turbulence Training for Abs, I put together ab routines using as little as three exercises in a circuit. One ab circuit that gives fast results involves the exercise ball jackknife followed by an exercise ball roll-out and then a side plank. This circuit gives you the benefits of dynamic abdominal contractions that you're used to when you do types of crunches, but with less stress on the low-back. The side plank at the end is for abdominal endurance helping you reduce your incidence of lower back pain. These exercises might be new to you, but you'll get very good results doing this circuit, as opposed to doing hundreds of crunches over and over again.

One other reason I avoid traditional ab exercises like crunches is because the worst thing you can possibly do for your low-back is to get up first thing in the morning and start doing sit-ups and crunches. When you sleep, fluid accumulates into your intervertebral discs making them larger than normal, and the ab flexion motion in sit-ups and crunches can compress these discs and by doing so, you greatly increase the chances of herniating a disc.

I learned this information from Dr. Stuart McGill, an expert in lower back health and performance. He sees a lot of disc herniations from spinal flexion that occurs when you round your lower back. You want to avoid rounding your lower back in all exercises, but that is the exact motion that occurs in crunches and sit-ups. So skip those exercises. The first thing for beginners to do to start improving their abdominal endurance and lower back health is to use exercises like the plank and side plank. Those aren't very exciting exercises, but they're critical in helping you avoid lower back trouble.

The plank exercise is done when you're supporting your body weight on your elbows and feet. Your body is in a straight line hovering above the ground, and you maintain that position, breathing normally and bracing your abs. You are going to hold that position, eventually working up to holding it for a full two minutes. Once you can do that, you've built excellent abdominal endurance that will protect your lower back.

For back health and performance, abdominal muscle endurance is more important than the ability to do hundreds and hundreds of crunches. Even with the total body ab exercises, I want you to focus on keeping your abs braced—and when I say "braced," I mean as if someone was going to punch you in the stomach. Dr. McGill also recommends you totally avoid any type of machine crunch found in most gyms; they just add to the dangers of spinal flexion and increase the chance for injury.

Advanced bodybuilders have to weigh the risks and benefits of building ab muscle and putting themselves through movements that aren't necessarily the safest for the lower back. But that's up to them, and the results they're after aren't really the same as Turbulence Training. More importantly, everyone basically has "abs," so the most important factor in being able to see your six-pack is to lose the belly fat that covers them up. You don't need to risk your lower back health doing hundreds of crunches and sit-ups to get a six-pack. For more home abdominal workouts, visit TurbulenceTrainingForAbs.com.

The Ultimate Fat-Burning Bodyweight Challenges

My popular bodyweight challenge workouts were created after I tried a program called the 300 Workout. A trainer for actors in the movie *The 300* designed the 300 Workout, and what he did was put together a really neat 300-repetition challenge for the actors to go through as a rite of passage. So, I took that concept and used it with bodyweight exercises only.

The bodyweight challenges that we're now using with *Men's Health* magazine and the Belly Off Program has a final 500-repetition challenge. That's five hundred repetitions of bodyweight exercises, but the program starts with a Bodyweight 100 challenge. You do two regular Turbulence Training workouts during the week and then you do a bodyweight challenge each Saturday for eight weeks. At the end of week one, the bodyweight challenge consists of one hundred repetitions, including squats, push-ups, chin-ups, and step-ups. In week two, you do the Bodyweight 100 twice. In week three, you do the Bodyweight 350. In week four, Bodyweight 350 plus another one hundred repetitions, and you follow that type of schedule, eventually working up to the Bodyweight 500.

Bodyweight 100 Workout

20 Prisoner Squats

20 Pushups

10 Jumps

10 Inverted Rows

20 Forward Lunges (10 reps per side)

15 Close-grip Pushups

5 Chin-ups or Inverted Rows

All exercises are done with as little rest as possible between each.

These bodyweight challenges have worked out really, really well because they add a competitive factor to a fat loss program, which is something that some people need to keep motivated and inspired to stick with the program. I've actually put together a Bodyweight 1000 program, which is much more advanced but uses the same principles. Depending on physical ability, injuries, or location, you can modify the bodyweight challenges to meet various fitness levels; but the best thing about the entire program is that with each week you'll get fitter, and the challenge will get harder to meet your improved fitness level.

People can get all of the bodyweight challenges and all of my bodyweight programs at TurbulenceTraining.com. In the deluxe bodyweight package, you will get the six-month Turbulence Training bodyweight manual, the Turbulence Training bodyweight manual for athletes, the Bodyweight 500, the Bodyweight 1000, and also the most advanced bodyweight exercise program that includes the hardest bodyweight exercises, including one-arm push-ups and one-leg squats.

We've actually had some people film their own workouts and put them on YouTube. One gentleman from the UK did the Bodyweight 500 and edited it down, put it to music, and created a three-minute video putting his time at the end. A couple of weeks later he made a new video in which he completed with the challenge in a faster time. I think this amply demonstrates how a wide variety of body weight exercises, including circuits, full body ab exercises, and the Bodyweight Challenge adds a new dimension to working out. Hopefully, you'll find it's a lot more fun this way, too!

Chapter Seven
Five Simple Nutrition Rules for Fat Burning

The great thing about starting a weight-loss program is that most of your initial results are going to come from nutrition. By making dietary changes at the start, it doesn't matter how little you're able to exercise; if you go from eating too much of the wrong food to the right amount of good food you're going to lose a lot of weight. The trick is not to make too many nutrition and exercise changes too fast. That's why I highly encourage the baby-step method. It helps you to avoid making any drastic lifestyle changes that you wouldn't normally be able to keep up with, and in the end, the nutrition part is the most difficult part of the new lifestyle. The baby-step method helps you build reasonable habits over time, while also avoiding digestive problems that come from a drastic change in diet.

Number One: Find out What You Are Eating

It's extremely important to find out how many calories you're eating because most people underestimate. That's one of the reasons why they aren't getting results and why they put weight on in the first place. I recommend a website called FitDay.com, where you can input the food that you eat every meal for every day. You should do this for an entire week at least in order to get a handle on how many calories you are taking in. For a lot of people this is a real shock because they think they're eating less than they are. It's easy to forget the bag of chips you grabbed, or the cookie you nibbled on, or the soda you had with lunch.

FitDay.com will not only show you how many calories you're getting but also the amount of carbohydrates, fat, protein, and fiber you're eating. And don't worry; you don't have to do this for the rest of your life. If you spend a week or two on this you'll have a much better idea of what you are eating and then can take that information to figure out what you should be eating. There are other Web sites and software products such as CalorieKing.com that can help you track your nutrition and give insight into just where those calories are coming from.

One common mistake is that most people don't take into account the number of calories they get from drinks. If you're drinking juices or sodas those can add up to a lot of calories, especially with the soda addiction that a lot of people around the world have. That simple can of soda has 150 calories! A bottle of beer has 150 calories, a shot of alcohol is around 100 calories, and a glass of wine is 100 to 150 calories. Most people also drink really large juices, which can add up. Same with sports and energy drinks. And the Starbucks Frappuccino drinks are notoriously high in calories. You can average 300 to 500 calories in one of those things, and it's all sugar. That stuff is going to help you gain weight or stop your fat loss progress very, very quickly.

There are several dangers when eating at restaurants, but the biggest is portion size and portion control. Restaurants serve such massive portions of food that most people, even nutritionists in one study, were fooled into eating more. We all get tricked by the large plate size, especially if you're anything like me and remember as a kid hearing your mom tell you to finish what's on your plate. If you put your meals on a smaller plate, you'll help reduce the amount of food you're eating.

When you're trying to lose body fat, nutrition experts for sake of simplicity often throw around the general recommendation of one gram of protein per pound of body weight, which is recommended by bodybuilders for gaining muscle. But if you're really overweight that can be inaccurate advice. What you want to aim for is about 150 to 200 grams of protein for men, and 100 to 150 grams of protein for women. Both of these amounts are more than enough.

Number Two: If You're Not Losing Fat, Eat Less

If you're gaining weight, one of the obvious things to do is to simply start eating less. If you're not gaining weight then you know how many calories you should eat approximately to maintain your weight. Alternatively, there are equations to help you estimate how many calories you need to eat—but again, these can overestimate your daily needs if you are an overweight individual. The simplest way to estimate how many calories you need to eat for weight loss is to take your body weight in pounds and multiply it by the number 11. But, again, that only works for the moderately overweight; the more you weigh the more it will overestimate your needs and stop you from losing fat.

Once you've learned from FitDay.com just how many calories you're taking in on average, start decreasing it by about twenty percent. If you are not losing weight, then focus on improving the quality of the food you're eating. The first place to start is by eliminating all sugar from your diet—sugary beverages are the first thing to go. Next, make sure to get rid of all processed carbohydrates, which would include most foods in a bag or box. Of course, that doesn't include whole grain rice, oatmeal, and things of that nature; but stuff like chips, crackers, breakfast cereals, and cookies are definitely off limits.

You also want to make sure that you're eliminating any foods containing trans fats, which are very unhealthy and lead to a lot of cardiovascular problems. Make sure you take a look at all the food packaging; food lobbying has allowed companies to get away with sneaking in trans fats. By law, as long as a product has less than 0.5 grams of trans fats per serving the label can claim that the product is trans fat-free, even though it is not. When many products include three to four servings per package, if you eat the entire package, you end up eating about two grams of trans fats. To avoid the murkiness of trans fat packaging, the best thing to do is to stick to whole, natural foods.

I would also avoid foods like rice cakes and other products that advertise themselves as low-fat or nonfat products. Although they might not have fat in them, they're often processed carbohydrates that can increase your blood sugar quite quickly and, as a result, drive your insulin up, which is a fat storage hormone. After your blood sugar increases quickly, it will also decrease quite quickly and that can result in hunger.

Likewise, meal replacement products like Slim-Fast are not the best way to lose weight because they are not much more than glorified chocolate beverages. Most people are going to have a hard time on that diet system because they are used to eating regular meals. To replace two out of three meals with a drink is going to be very tough to maintain in the long term. It certainly would not be as satisfying a program as eating a normal sized meal that consisted of whole, natural foods.

Number Three: Eat Whole Natural Foods

The best types of food to eat are those that haven't been changed in any form. That means lots of fruits and vegetables. I like people to try a new fruit and vegetable every week or every month. There's probably a lot in the grocery store that you've never tried before, and you might be surprised by what you like.

As you may have read, fish, flax seed oil, and nuts such as almonds, walnuts, and pecans are great sources of healthy fat. Don't be put off by the fact that you are eating some fat; there is such thing as good fat. Almonds are great because they provide monounsaturated fat and a lot of fiber. In fact, one study found that increasing almond consumption actually *helped* in weight loss. I generally recommend one ounce of raw almonds for snacks midmorning and mid-afternoon, and since there are about twenty-two almonds in an ounce, that's a satisfying snack.

The most important thing for fat loss nutrition is to plan ahead. Most people have great intentions when they start the week, but if they don't plan ahead and prepare their meals they end up in a lot of situations where there's nothing but the vending machine. Planning ahead and packing fruits, vegetables, and nuts to have at your desk or in your car when hunger strikes is going to be a lot easier than pulling into a drive-thru and trying to find something healthy on the menu. Even if you do, there are probably a lot more added calories that you're not taking into account because of the oil or butter that the food is cooked in.

It's difficult to just jump right in to this healthy food lifestyle, so fall back on the baby-step method. Just like trying one new fruit or vegetable each day, try to make one improvement to your diet. Eat slightly better today than you did yesterday. Add an apple or a serving of broccoli to your lunch. Cut out a sugary snack or beverage. If you're only eating two servings of vegetables, on the next day, eat three, and then four. It's too intimidating to ask beginners to switch entirely over to fruits and vegetables with no processed foods all in one day—not mention how hard that would be on their stomach and digestive system. If you improve your diet by one aspect every day, it won't be long before it turns into a habit, which is the first step to a healthy lifestyle.

Number Four: Give Yourself One Reward Meal Per Week

You may have heard the term "cheat meal" or "cheat day," but I'd rather talk about in this terms of "reward" because you're rewarding yourself for a job well done. Cheating implies that you're doing something you shouldn't be doing, and it also gives you that idea that you can eat whatever they want. A reward meal is more about eating foods that you like but eating them in moderate quantities. Instead of eating an entire pizza, you should just have a few slices.

If you want to get maximum fat loss results from your nutrition program then you should use what Dr. John Berardi calls the "90% compliance rule," in that you need to eat ninety percent compliant during the week for maximum results. Most people think that they're eating perfect, but if you look at their nutrition compliance, they're probably at about seventy or seventy-five percent. You'll start getting good results once you hit eighty percent but if you want to get maximum results you have to get up to ninety percent. What that really means is you have to eat right ninety percent of the time, so ninety percent of your meals need to be according to your plan.

The easiest way to determine your nutrition compliance is to draw out a chart for seven days and then make a box for each meal down the side of the page. If you're going to eat according to the six small meals per day rule then you have forty-two boxes over the course of an entire week. To achieve ninety percent compliance, that requires thirty-eight of those boxes to be checked off as eating according to plan. That gives you three reward snacks over the course of the week and one reward meal—but they're not all giant fast-food meals. They might just be snacks or something that you miss. And don't be fooled, it's better to have one single reward meal rather than an entire reward day. As my nutritionist friend John Alvino says, "Your reward meal starts when you sit down to the table and ends as soon as you get up."

That means not going back for seconds or thirds or coming back for a midnight snack. You have your reward meal and then you move on and get back on plan.

By avoiding binge eating, you'll avoid what I call the Cardio Confessional—pigging out on the weekend and then coming into the gym on Monday trying to work off all the calories you consumed. The Friday after Thanksgiving is notorious for this, as is the day after New Years. First of all, it would take two or more hours to work off the number of calories that are typically involved in a binge, and, secondly, it's just not healthy or effective. In fact, it borders on exercise bulimia. You shouldn't feel bad about your reward meal because you've earned it, and you definitely shouldn't go into the gym thinking that need you need to do your penance.

The most important benefit your reward meal provides is psychological in that it gives you something to look forward to over the course of the week, a reward for sticking to your plan and doing all that hard work. That's not to say that your plan should be so strict and regimented that you hate every minute of it. You should be looking for ways to eat healthy and enjoy it, but you can still have that pizza with your family on Saturday night or that dessert on Sunday at your parents' house. In the short term it is a reward, but through the course of the week, it's an incentive to stay on plan and eat properly.

Number Five: Plan Ahead

At least once a week you should sit down and plan out your meals for the next few days ahead. This is called the "plan, shop, and prepare" method. Plan your shopping list, go to the grocery store, and then come home and prepare as much of your food as possible and put it in individual containers to take to work. It is best to do this on a free day, such as Saturday or Sunday. Give yourself an hour-and-a-half to two hours to do all of this, and if necessary mass cook chicken breasts or other types of protein. You can then freeze that food so that you can take it to work in a cooler or in Tupperware. No matter how you do it, by planning ahead you can eat right and avoid the dreaded vending machine or an overpriced restaurant without any healthy options.

When people make the decision to start eating right they always have great intentions, but, in practice, things go wrong because life is so stressful. You may think you're going to get up at seven a.m. to prepare your food for that day, but chances are you'll get up at seven-thirty and the next thing you know you're at work with no breakfast and no lunch planned, going to the vending machine or the doughnut shop or Starbucks, consuming calories that aren't on your plan and then going out for lunch with colleagues who aren't into the same healthy lifestyle. If you plan and prepare, all you have to do is grab and go from the fridge. You're going to be so much better off, and the nutrition part of the program is going to be so much easier.

The most important thing to remember is that you cannot out-train a bad diet. It doesn't matter how intense your workout is, if you are eating more calories than you should, and the wrong kinds of food, all of your hard work will be for nothing.

Here are the rules one more time:

✓ Find out what you are eating.

✓ If you are not losing fat, eat less.

✓ Eat whole, natural foods.

✓ Give yourself one reward meal per week.

✓ Plan ahead.

When you grab your free gift at turbulencetraining.com/freegift, you will also get a nutrition plan from Dr. Chris Mohr, a registered dietician, and it's very simple. Dr. Mohr's plan follows the whole natural foods guidelines, and also helps overweight men and women determine how much protein and how many calories they need instead of just sticking to rules that apply only to lean people. He outlines plenty of whole, natural foods, fruits and vegetables, carbohydrate sources, and protein sources that most people have never thought of. The report is *The Turbulence Training for Fat Loss Nutrition Guidelines*, and it is the best place to get a safe, sound, and effective nutrition guide for fat loss. You'll get this report as a bonus when you claim your FREE one month Turbulence Training membership at TurbulenceTraining.com/freegift.

Chapter Eight
The Top Five Fat Loss Myths

Myth #1: Early Morning Cardio on an Empty Stomach Burns Fat Faster

Many people have gotten this idea from bodybuilding magazines, but it doesn't necessarily mean that it's true. Others get their information from people that look the part in the gym. If someone has bulging muscles and washboard abs, it is reasonable to believe what they tell you; but what they don't tell you is how much time they spend in the gym and what other substances they might be taking. Just because someone has a body that you admire doesn't mean you should admire how they got it.

There is no harm in training first thing in the morning. It certainly is convenient to do it earlier than later, but it is not a magic bullet. It doesn't matter if you train first thing in the morning, at lunch, after work, or after the kids go to bed. The time of your workout really does not make a difference so long as you're working out on a consistent basis. Just train when you can, and more importantly, train consistently and correctly.

A lot of people get what I call *paralysis by analysis,* meaning that they hear so much information that they end up over thinking everything and not taking action. So long as you stick to the two basic principles of consistency and intensity, combined with a healthy diet of whole natural foods, you are sure to get the results you want.

Myth #2: You Have To Do Cardio in the Fat Burning Zone

A lot of fitness experts have written about the fat burning zone and at what percentage of exercise intensity you are burning the most body fat, as it pertains to calories. They claim that around sixty percent of your maximum exertion, which is based on the amount of oxygen you consume during exercise, is proportionally when you are burning the most amount of fat, at least compared to proteins and carbohydrates. At eighty percent, for example, you would be burning more calories, but proportionately less of them would come from fat. Therefore, working out at sixty percent exertion is better than eighty percent, right?

Wrong. The more calories you burn the better, no matter where they come from. According to the principle behind the fat burning zone, you burn more fat calories sitting on the couch than you do running—at least proportionally. Obviously, people aren't losing the fat by sitting on the couch, so the fat burning zone is just a complete misinterpretation of a scientific principal that doesn't really apply to getting results.

Even if you start to exercise and increase your intensity up to the sixty percent of this magical fat burning zone area, it's still not going to make as great of an impact as if you burned more calories at a higher intensity of exercise. It just doesn't make sense, which is exactly why it's a myth.

Activity	Calories Burned	Fat % Percentage	Calories from Fat
Watching TV for 30 Minutes	50	70	35
Jogging for 30 Minutes	150	60	90
Running for 30 Minutes	300	40	120

*from http://pinoyfitness.com/?p=8

The chart above demonstrates why the fat burning zone is a convincing, albeit, misguided myth. The most important thing to realize here is that the actual workout is just a small component of your daily calorie burning. The most important thing to remember is that a light workout doesn't boost your metabolism after training, but a short burst exercise program, such as Turbulence Training, does.

Myth #3: You Have To Do Cardio for Twenty Minutes Before You Burn Fat

Someone somewhere along the line came up with this one; I don't even have a scientific explanation for it. At all times we're burning body fat, and at all times we're burning carbohydrates. We're even burning a little bit of protein. Think of it this way. There are three taps that are open all the time: fat, protein, and carbohydrates. When you exercise, you open the carbohydrate and fat taps quite a bit. It's not like you ever shut those taps off for anything—even if you're sprinting, you're still burning a little bit of fat when most people would say that you're burning only carbohydrates. But no matter how short or long your workout might be, you were burning fat from the moment you started—and before. We never stop burning fat, ever.

Myth #4: You Can Boost Your Metabolism with Supplements

One misconception is that caffeine boosts your metabolism, but I've also heard that fish oil, protein, CLA, and green tea will do it, too. As with the fat burning zone, this myth comes from a distortion of science. Green tea, for example, was shown to increase the daily energy expenditure of young men by eighty calories per day. Now, that's great news for the people who make supplements because they can put that claim on their label, but what that doesn't take into account is that people's bodies adapt to a stimulus. If there is any benefit to taking a particular supplement, by the end of the week, your body has adjusted to the chemical and no longer reacts to it. And that's why, as a recent study showed, that taking Green Tea supplements for 12 weeks did not cause any fat loss. Most supplements seem to be nothing more than glorified caffeine pills.

Let's think of this another way. Say for example that green tea extract actually did help you burn an additional eighty calories per day. It is agreed upon by most trainers that one pound of fat is equal to 3,500 calories. Even if the supplement worked as intended, then it would take nearly a month and half to lose one pound!

Unfortunately, you'll find big promises from supplements in every magazine, and it is very difficult to avoid the allure of the quick fixes that supplements present. Supplements make you think, "Why work out when you can take a pill?" And as long as there are people who aren't willing to work for their results, there will always be a product claiming to work miracles.

Unlike these "miracle" supplements, research repeatedly shows that both strength training and interval training can help boost your metabolism and burn fat. In one study, women did a strength training session with eight repetitions per exercise and had a significant increase in their post-exercise metabolism. This is just another example of how short burst training will burn more calories and more fat. These are proven results that no diet pill can compete with.

Myth #5: You Can't Gain Muscle and Lose Fat at the Same Time

According to scientific theory there's absolutely no way that someone can gain muscle and lose fat at the same time, so let's take a look at the research to see where theories end and the real world begins.

A study from Purdue University included men and women with an average age of just over sixty, found that the subjects, on average, gained four pounds of muscle and lost four pounds of fat over a twelve-week strength-training-only program. They didn't do cardio and they weren't even asked to change their diets. They simply added a three-day-per-week circuit type strength training program, and the subjects gained muscle and lost fat. This shows you how much of a myth #5 really is, but it also proves that it's possible to get results at any age.

The idea that you can't gain muscle and lose fat at the same time may sound reasonable within a classroom, but it doesn't hold up in the real world where people are gaining muscle and losing fat with scientifically proven training programs. I have so many testimonials from people using the Turbulence Training programs that there is just no more reason to believe that you can't gain muscle and lose fat at the same time.

How to Handle Paralysis by Analysis

As I mentioned earlier, one of the biggest dangers your training might face is paralysis by analysis. There is just so much information out there, and so much that isn't true, that when you face all the facts it can be overwhelming. Hopefully, I've cleared away some of the myths and misconceptions and the path to fat loss seems a little more clear. You can discover more fat loss myths at DietDebunker.com.

Here are a few things to remember:

✓ You don't have to do cardio in the morning or on an empty stomach to burn fat.

✓ The Fat Burning Zone is a distortion of facts that will not lead to the best results.

✓ You don't have to do cardio for twenty minutes before you start burning fat.

✓ Supplements that promise to boost your metabolism are rarely effective, and never work in the long term.

✓ It is possible to gain muscle and lose fat at the same time.

Chapter Nine
The Forgotten Secret to Fat Loss Success

Social support is the most neglected aspect of fat loss programs, but it can actually be the most important factor in your success. Social support is simply about having friends, family, and co-workers who understand the program and are willing to give encouragement along the way. One study shows that when people go to a gym with a workout partner who is succeeding in weight loss, then they have a greater chance of succeeding in weight loss as well. Unfortunately, if they went to the gym with someone who didn't lose weight, then they didn't have such a great chance of losing fat either. The lesson, then, is to surround yourself with people who have the same types of goals, who are getting the same types of results, and who are supportive in nature.

If you don't have an entire network behind you, it's still vitally important to have one or two people that you can e-mail, call, or communicate with by Internet forum. You can share the rough patches that you're going through and get feedback from those who may have been in the same situation. That's what social support is all about, and it's possible that some of the best weight loss support may actually come from professionals. Make sure you can go to your doctor, nutritionist, or personal trainer and be held accountable. You may also want to try starting a weight loss challenge at work or join some type of fitness forum on the Internet.

Your support network can also act as a resource for practical information such as what snacks to take on the road or how to exercise when you're away from the gym. There is a social support forum at TTMembers.com, and I'm always struck by how people have come together from around the world to be supportive, almost like family, and help each other. One group going through the twelve-week program was made up of about half a dozen people from Australia and New Zealand, over one hundred Americans, several Canadians, a handful of folks from the UK, and even men from both Bahrain and Russia. So while folks slept in North America, members from the UK, New Zealand, and Australia would be posting helpful tips and encouraging notes to one another. This has turned out to be a very motivational source of support to start their day with. When you grab your free gift at TurbulenceTraining.com/freegift, you'll get a one month free Turbulence Training membership.

In the forum, if someone goes a day or two without posting an update on their progress, other members will start to check-in and send messages asking if everything is okay. "Are you back on track? Did you fall off track? How can we help?" And that gets people feeling a little bit guilty that they're not keeping up and that others are making an effort to check in on them. It really gives them a kick in the butt to get back on track, even if they went missing for three or four days and everyone thought they were going to quit. Instead, these people are brought back in because they don't want to let other people down.

Positive encouragement is the best kind, but sometimes you need tough love, too. For example, one person on our membership forum continued to justify her eating habits because she had a lot of bad days at work. Once in a while the other members had to tell her to quit making excuses and just stick to the program. Most adults are fairly autonomous in their jobs and personal lives, and I think we forget what it's like to have someone looking over our shoulders, pushing, and just how much we can accomplish by having someone else to answer to.

Goal-Setting

I encourage all Turbulence Training clients to set three short-term and three long-term goals when they first start the program and to review these goals on a regular basis. Research shows that people who set goals have more success in all areas of life.

Beginners should set goals that will help them make those baby steps to fat loss. One baby step is planning your meals in advance. That's a process goal, rather than an outcome goal. An outcome goal would be to lose five pounds of fat in the first week. But since you don't have complete control of how much fat you lose, it's better to set process goals, such as "I'm going to go to the gym three times this week," or "I'm going to be active on my off days" or "I'm going to spend an hour and a half preparing my food on the weekends." Those are three short-term process goals that will help a beginner get off to an incredibly great start.

Advanced fat loss folks might have a goal of doing three interval training sessions per week or setting a personal best in every workout. Like my friend, world-famous strength coach Jay Ferruggia says, I believe that setting personal records in workouts helps people get better results. If you are at an advanced level, you might also want to set process goals for helping you stick to your ninety percent nutrition compliance.

I also use a process called, "reverse goal setting" to help people set short term goals in addition to long term goals.

Reverse goal setting is a unique way of setting goals that starts with the end point in mind. For example, if you know you're going to do a twelve-week transformation program and you want to lose eighteen pounds of belly fat, then you start at the eighteen pounds of belly fat on day eighty-four and work your way back. So you know you need to be at about seventeen pounds by eleven weeks, fifteen by ten weeks, and so on and so forth just working your way back. This way you can stick to your schedule and be more realistic, rather than expecting to lose five pounds after week one, or ten pounds after week two. If you goal-set like that, you won't meet the goals because you set them too big at the start. By reverse goal setting you can adjust on the fly as you work towards the long-term goal.

Taking Measurements

Measurements are really important because of objective comparison. A lot of people that do not take measurements often end up with an improper assessment of how they're doing. They think that they're not losing fat or they think that they're getting big and bulky, but they haven't taken any measurements and they're only going by what they see or think they see in the mirror. If you take measurements, then the difference between week two and week six is quantifiable; it may even become a point of pride. Measurements also help you to identify what works and what doesn't. So, for example, if you try a program of cardio only and then switch over to the Turbulence Training program, and you've made measurements all throughout each program, now you can accurately assess how your body responds to each program and you can determine which program is best for you. I strongly recommend keeping track of your nutrition as well, because if you ever find yourself running into a plateau, you can just go back to your training book and identify, "Well, when I did this program I had my greatest results. It's been six months since I did that program. So, maybe I'll jump back and see if I can kick-start my fat loss."

This is really helpful for the transformation contest especially; it's so motivating to see the changes from week zero to week twelve. It's really inspiring, not only for yourself, but also for the other people in the contest or your network of support.

The most important thing to start with is bodyweight and also limb circumferences, so use a measuring tape around your upper arm, your chest, your waist, your hips, your thighs. That way you can monitor how much smaller you get over time. Bodyweight is great and important to take, but it doesn't necessarily tell the whole story.

In addition to that, you should also take pictures from the front, side, and back so that you can compare your pictures over time. Also, if possible, get your body fat measurement taken. The best and simplest way to do it is to have your body fat taken by a professional trainer with skin-fold calipers and multiple measurement sites. In fact, I truly believe that a good trainer should be able to eyeball your body fat. I know that I can do it just with pictures that people send in to me on the Turbulence Training message board. I can tell exactly, within one or two percent, what their actual body fat measurement is.

A more common way to determine body fat is by using handheld electronic body fat scales, or the Tanita body fat scales. You hold the scale in your hand and it tells you your body fat; these are a reliable indicator of how well you are improving over time. For the scale to be reliable, the measurement should be taken under the same conditions each time: the same time of day, the same food eaten, and the same activity as the day before. If done correctly, the measurement should be able to track your progress, but most of the time they do underestimate your body fat percentage. If you hear some guy who says he has four percent body fat according to body fat scale, unless he's a professional bodybuilder whose in contest condition, there's no way he has four percent body fat. So, take claims of extremely low body fat levels with a grain of salt. Body fat measurements can be used to accurately track your changes over time, but they are definitely not as easy to measure as stepping on a scale or taking the circumference of your waist.

Typically, I like people to weigh in weekly, although there's something to be said for checking even more frequently. People do make the mistake of worrying too much when the scale rebounds; sometimes the scale will be a little bit wild or you might find that you gained a couple of pounds over the weekend. But, in reality, it's next to impossible for someone to gain two pounds of body fat over a weekend because one pound of fat is 3,500 calories, so that means you would have had to eaten 7,000 calories more than you needed. It's more likely that you gained two pounds of fluid either from drinking more or eating more salt or carbohydrates. That's a lot more likely, after all, you would have to eat the equivalent of fourteen Big Macs in addition to your regular meals to gain two pounds of fat over the weekend.

Staying Consistent

Being accountable helps people be consistent, and as I said at the start of the book, consistency is one of the most important things in a fat loss program. It's better than worrying about all the minutiae, such as when the best time of day to work out is or exactly how much protein you need down to the specific gram. As long as you're consistent, you're going to be getting great results. Being accountable will do that for you because you don't want to let somebody else down.

It's nearly impossible to lose a lot of body fat on your own. If you try to be a maverick you're going to end up with a lot more frustration and a lot less weight loss than if you had someone to talk to and maybe get a pat on the back from when you think you're doing worse than you are. A lot of people are also pretty hard on themselves and don't acknowledge the good things they've done, only focusing on the mistakes they've made. Accountability enables other people to build you up when you deserve it, as well as encourage you when you're slipping.

I recommend that you look for some type of positive fitness forum in which people are generally out there to help one another and there's a sense of community and family. Obviously with Turbulence Training, the best place to go is TTMembers.com because people are going through the same workouts and using the same nutrition program; therefore, they will have the same ups and downs as you.

Chapter Ten
The Five Step Quick-Start Guide to Burning Belly Fat

Step #1: Stop Boring Cardio, Start Short Burst Exercise

Interval training takes about half the time and gives you more results than long cardio workouts. If you're doing a lot of cardio, the best thing to do is to switch long, slow, lower-intensity exercise over to short bursts of harder exercise, alternating with easy active recovery, so that you start to get the benefits of the more intense exercise method that is interval training. Some of my clients have come to me doing five to seven hours of cardio per week, and we're cutting them down to only one hour of interval training per week—three sessions of twenty minutes. You can save several hours per week in training time and less time driving to the gym, too.

For beginner, intermediate, and advanced exercisers alike who want more fat loss-specific interval training workouts, you can try the Turbulence Training workouts by visiting TurbulenceTraining.com/freegift.

Step #2: Work Out at Home with Minimal Equipment

The only thing that's needed is a small investment in a mini home gym setup, including adjustable dumbbells, an exercise bench, an exercise ball, and a pull-up bar. If you want to and can afford it, you can also use a squat rack, a barbell, and a bench press. Most people only have about one hundred square feet in their basement or their garage, however, and can still set up a very effective fat burning factory there with the minimal equipment.

If you don't have the space to do cardio at home you can do your exercise outside. Hills are a great place to do running, walking, and speed walking for your interval training; you can take your bike out as well. And of course, bodyweight circuits are an excellent way to do interval-type training.

Step #3: Change Your Workouts Regularly

The first principle of having a successful workout is **variety**. That means you want to have a variety of different exercises, sets, and reps in your programs. You also want to have variety in your interval training—different interval workouts for workout A and workout B within the same program—so that you're not doing the same thing over and over again.

The second principle, **intensity**, means to increase intensity of your training. That's the biggest thing for most people, who tend to be doing a lot of slow, low-intensity exercise. Even their strength training is low-intensity, often using a weight that they could do twenty or thirty reps with but doing only fifteen. Once you switch over to high-intensity strength training and interval training from light weights and slow cardio, you're going to get a lot of fat burning results in a short amount of time.

The **change** principle is that every four weeks you need to change up your workouts. You're not doing the same thing for longer than four weeks. By changing, you're always going to be putting a new stress on your body and, therefore, getting more results in the same amount of workout time.

The most important thing is that you get your information from a professional trainer. One of the biggest mistakes I see is people trying to design their own workouts. Generally, when they do that they only include the stuff that they're good at or like to do. But the thing is, you'll probably get the most results out of the exercises that you find hard to do. For example, most of my clients love doing pressing exercises but don't like dumbbell rows or split squats because they're difficult. And yet, those are the exercises that are probably going to give them more results.

Make sure that you have a trainer design a total body workout that address all the muscles as needed so that you're not doing more chest pressing than you are rowing and ending up with structural problems. The professional advice, just like with anything in life from an accountant to a lawyer, should come from someone who has the expertise. If you haven't already grabbed the Turbulence Training package, get your copy from TurbulenceTraining.com/freegift, and then you'll get added to the Turbulence Training membership site where you will be getting the fat loss information you need from a professional. You also get a new workout every month so that you don't have to think about changing your workout program on your own; you can just go in and follow the instructions. That's the most important thing because that saves you time. It also gets you results faster because it's a professionally designed program guaranteed to get you results.

Step #4: Work Out Harder, Not Longer

If you workout with more intensity, you can get more results in less time. It may sound like an oxymoron, but try to push yourself conservatively. As with overuse injuries and in terms of general workout safety, it is very difficult to lose weight when you are injured.

For interval training intensity, I like to use a subjective level of intensity, so interval training should be done at an eight or nine out of ten. A six out of ten intensity level is what you'd regularly do your cardio at, so interval training is a couple notches higher than that. A ten out of ten intensity is what I call "running for your life." You don't want to do this with interval training; you're always going to hold back a little bit, but you're going to work very hard just the same. Again, this will take a little trial-and-error, especially if you're using different interval durations to find out exactly what intensity you can use for thirty to sixty seconds.

For strength training, if you're a beginner and have never done weights before the only thing you can do is to start as light as possible and use trial-and-error. If you've used five pounds for an exercise and you find that it's really, really easy, just do a couple repetitions, put the weights back and try ten pounds, and work your way up that way. There are no hard and fast rules as to what beginners should use for any certain exercise, so you just have to increase your intensity over time. The best thing to do to shortcut all this is to hire a trainer for one session to help you find out the right amount of weight that you should use for each exercise, and also to check proper form.

By increasing the quality of each exercise session you can actually get more results in terms of burning fat and building muscle. Somewhere along the line this idea came about that you have to be in the gym every day doing more and more work. Nobody thought to work out harder, not longer. But recent research is starting to show that increasing intensity is the best way to get more results in less time. You still have to work hard and be consistent, but you aren't going to be in the gym for as many hours as you were before.

By doing this increased intensity of exercise, you're going to be putting more turbulence on your body; what I found is that the magic happens *outside* the training session, during the recovery. This makes sense if you look at the same approach that bodybuilders take. They know that when they go to the gym and lift weights that they aren't going to come out bigger as soon as the workout is over. It takes several days for those muscles to recover and repair, eventually making them bigger and stronger. It's the same analogy with fat loss. You want to do hard work and put turbulence on your muscles during the training instead of worrying about how many calories you burn, because it's during the time after training when your metabolism is increased from that workout, that you'll burn more calories and lose more fat. Turbulence Training takes the big picture approach to fat loss instead of worrying so much about the little details within the workout. I just want you to focus on consistent, high-intensity exercise.

More trainers are starting to talk about high-intensity interval training and strength training, supersets, and circuit training as a way to build a better body. You're going to start seeing that in a lot more in magazines, especially *Men's Health* magazine and also on Web sites. But Turbulence Training is the first program to combine non-competing supersets, interval training, and bodyweight exercises to help you get fat loss results in the shortest amount of time possible. Since then a lot of people have copied the approach, but none of the programs have had the same sort of magic as mine does. The reason for that is because I've been doing this for so long and trained so many clients that I've built up a warehouse of information. Thousands and thousands of people are using Turbulence Training, including over five thousand men using the *Men's Health* Belly-Off Program.

Step #5: Eat Whole, Natural Foods

Unfortunately, too many people are eating so poorly these days that they couldn't eat any worse. With so many processed carbohydrates, sugary drinks, trans fats, and fast food, it seems like we're living in a perfect world for fat storage. Even if you're smart enough to not eat a large quantity of this kind of stuff, most food is so dense with calories that it is difficult not to overeat. Eating processed foods also causes blood sugar to rapidly increase and then decrease, causing your hunger to return rapidly, leading you to eat more processed food and thus repeating the cycle. Breaking this cycle by eating nutrient dense foods that contain fiber and protein to suppress appetite results in eating less and losing fat.

If you are at the extreme end of the poor eating scale and make a change to eat more fruits, vegetables, healthy fats through nuts and fish, and high-quality protein sources, then you're going to end up with rapid, healthy weight loss. You'll also have more mental energy, you'll be less tired after eating, you'll be more alert, and you'll feel like you will be able to get more things done. Hopefully, you'll also be more inclined to work out with this new energy, and that will increase your rate of fat loss.

The best thing to do is to get simple, safe, proven effective advice, and that's what Dr. Chris Mohr has given us in the *Turbulence Training for Fat Loss Nutrition Guidelines*. He maps out a simple meal plan system that can be achieved by any man or woman. It doesn't take a lot of time and it doesn't require any extreme approaches to losing fat. It just shows you how to eat healthy foods in the correct amount.

Cooling Down

One of the greatest hurdles that beginners face is the idea that more is not necessarily better. With long hours on the treadmill, you'll find nothing but wasted time, battered joints, and disappointing results. That said, Turbulence Training is not the easiest program out there. It requires a level of dedication that, though brief, is more intense than what most people are used to. But it is through this intensity that you find a success whose benefits extend beyond your shrinking waistline.

The important thing to remember is that it doesn't matter how old or out of shape you are, and it doesn't matter what kind of body type you have; although it's tough, Turbulence Training works for everyone. There are just too many examples of people who've achieved great physiques for you to think that you can't do it. As long as you make up your mind to commit yourself, Turbulence Training offers you better results, more free time, and a life applicable regimen that is easily maintained. The only thing left to do now is to get started. So good luck, and I'll see you on the Turbulence Training forums!

Chapter 11
Turbulence Training Members Speak Out

In the past few years, I've developed such a passion for the program that it feels like I could go on forever talking about it. Fortunately, I'm not the only one because people all over the world who want to tell me how great the system is treating them have contacted me. What I've got here is a collection of letters and e-mails that I have received over the past few years. These are real people who have had their lives changed by Turbulence Training and the transformation contest. If you go to TurbulenceTraining.com or TransformationContest.com you will find these stories and many more, including some really great before and after pictures.

The great thing about these stories is that they demonstrate how Turbulence Training works for everyone. From the father of two to the fireman, from the busy moms approaching forty or fifty to the young single woman just out of college, all these people have gotten great results and were so happy that they just had to write to tell me all about it. These are real people getting real results, sharing their true stories that I hope will inspire you as much as they do me. The Turbulence Training program will work for everyone—if you are willing to make the commitment. Here are the stories of people who made the decision and never went back.

"I am a forty-eight-year-old woman who has been on some sort of diet plan since 1987 (that's when my son was born) I've tried all sorts of exercise programs: Curves, The Firm, 6 weeks, and numerous Beach Body programs, not to mention Atkins, Slim Fast, Nutrisystem, low fat, low carb, low calorie, etc. You name it, I've tried it—and probably bought it!

"Three weeks ago I stumbled across Craig's "Dark Side of Cardio." But wait, here it is three weeks later and I've lost ten pounds! (I started at 173.) My clothes are looser! What is happening here? A program that actually delivers! A program without false promises! A program that doesn't make you workout five to seven days a week but only three times a week for forty-five minutes! I've got to tell you, I was certainly skeptical because of past history, but WOW, I can't believe this. I tried on a skirt that I couldn't get past my hips last winter and I wore it today! I love this program; it's fast, fun, and complete. Thank you, Craig, for helping me with my dream."

Kelley Howard

"My twelve-week Turbulence Training transformation started on January 7, 2008. I felt frustrated and out-of-shape. After working a desk job for a few years my clothes weren't fitting anymore and I was desperate to get my old body back. I had spent thousands of dollars on a personal trainer (which I am still paying off to this day), tried numerous fad diets, was reading fitness literature with conflicting messages, and was spending forty-five minutes to an hour every morning on an elliptical machine thinking it would burn body fat and give me the fit look I wanted. None of it offered me a solution that was livable. I only ended up worn out, in debt, frustrated, and above all confused.

"When I discovered Turbulence Training on the Web and realized it only involved doing three workouts a week with weight training and about twenty minutes of cardio, it sounded like a dream. With that regimen I could reclaim so much of my free time, while getting the results so many TT members were seeing. I had nothing to lose and immediately purchased the Turbulence Training program. I joined the transformation contest because I knew I needed some accountability to get myself on track, and above all, it looked like fun. My goals for the end of the twelve weeks were to increase strength and lose body weight, fat, and inches.

"Over the twelve weeks I followed a reduced calorie diet (following Dr. Mohr's guidelines) trying to eat as clean as I could at all times. I used the TT for Fat Loss Intermediate workout, the TT for Women Beginner/Intermediate workout, the TT for Women Advanced Workout, and finished with the TT for Fat Loss 2K8 workout. The contest definitely gave me motivation but ultimately turned into so much more. The support I found from the TT community was amazing: everyone sharing tips and encouraging one another—it was really an incredible experience. I learned so much about training and nutrition through the TT manuals, Craig's advice and interviews, and other TT users. When there was temptation to slack on my nutrition or skip a workout, Craig and the fellow TT'ers were always there to remind me to 'Stay strong!' When I made gains in my workouts, like being able to finally do decline push-ups, the forum was there to cheer me on.

"Today, so much of the body self-consciousness I have always felt has slowly faded. I'm back into my size fours and I finally have taken charge of my health. I feel confident and fantastic. Turbulence Training has armed me with an arsenal of fat-burning workouts that really work and make the most effective use of my time! I know now that being fit isn't impossible. I can work my desk job and live a fitness lifestyle. The proof lies in the numbers....

January 7, 2008

weight: 140 lbs

percent body fat: 23.7%

waist: 27.5"

hip: 39"

March 30, 2008

weight: 131 lbs

percent body fat: 19%

waist: 25.25"

hip: 37.25"

These were just the first twelve weeks of the rest of my life. Thanks, Craig!"

Laura Meyer

"I've done just about everything from Turbo Jam and P90X to trying to piece together my own workout, but I didn't get the results I've seen with Turbulence Training. My problem has always been my legs. No matter what I tried I have never been able to reduce the size of my thighs. I've tried the numerous leg routines featured in countless women's fitness magazines, but nothing worked. But with Turbulence Training I began to notice that my thighs looked smoother and more toned. Even my calf muscles were a lot shapelier. I started seeing these changes about three weeks into the program, *and* I got these results without killing myself. The workouts are efficient and a lot of fun. I recommend this program to any woman who is struggling to lose that stubborn lower body fat. It is truly a godsend. A heartfelt thank you."

Andrea Dunham

"It's been about six weeks since I started the initial program and have moved onto the women's four-week program with fantastic results. I really appreciate how comprehensive the manuals are, with detailed pictures and instructions. Best money I ever spent! I've also used the nutritional guidelines, which are so easy to follow. The result? The love handles on my back have disappeared and my stomach is much flatter, my arms are more toned, and even my legs look thinner! To say I am happy is an understatement! Even at the two- to three-week mark my husband was commenting that I'd lost weight, and since then people have really noticed that my shape is changing. Every week people are asking, 'Have you lost more weight?' My body fat is really shifting and the best bit is that it takes far less time than going to the gym, giving me much more time for me! It also feels great to take control of my workouts!

"I'm looking forward to the next few weeks and months as I continue on the various workouts to see how much more my body can change. It's great that there are so many workouts to keep the body challenged! Thank you for providing such proven workouts for poor misguided people like me!"

Nicole Bailey

"I felt fat. My XL clothes were tight, and I had just bought size forty jeans (a first in my life). Despite all this, I didn't do anything about it, until my three-year-old son asked me why I had "big boobies." I can't think of a more embarrassing question a son can ask his dad. I have three kids and my oldest is only four, so I didn't have a lot of time to dedicate to getting in shape. I thought it took ninety minutes a day, six days a week to get into shape. In addition, I've never been able to stick with a nutrition or workout plan for longer than a month.

"Then I read about Turbulence Training. I found great support from Craig and the rest of the great people in the TTMembers.com forums. As I progressed further into my twelve-week transformation, I found that my body was losing fat extremely quickly; but more importantly, my mindset was changing. I found myself looking forward to the workouts, and looking forward to eating good foods. I never worked out more than three days a week. In fact, I had overworked myself at the beginning and worked out only once in the first eighteen days of the contest, and it showed: I only lost two pounds. For the last sixty-six days, I really started following the Turbulence Training program to the letter, and ended up losing thirty-two pounds in that time. This is the first time in my life I feel like I am in decent shape. Before the contest, I couldn't do any chin-ups; now I can do almost four. Before, I had trouble bench-pressing fifty-five-pound dumbbells. Now, I use seventy-five-pound dumbbells.

"Finally, the bodyweight 200 circuit that I did as my first TT workout took me nearly thirty minutes to complete, and made me feel like I was about to die afterward. Today, I did the exact same workout in under thirteen minutes and felt ready to do another couple rounds.

"Turbulence Training works. I am proof of that. But I'm also proof that it only works if you put the principles into practice. Once I read the book, I intellectually knew how I could lose fat. Now that I've followed the program, I know how to lose fat."

Steve Hays

"Being a father of twin boys, I was overweight at 217 pounds more than a year ago; and seeing my kids grow up right before my eyes—it just hit me. Craig's down to earth, straightforward personality in his books and user-friendly Web site really attracted me the most. He really does support you with answers that are very helpful in his book and on his site. All you need is a few dumbbells, a bench, a stability ball, and you're set. I'm now at 167 pounds and ten percent body fat, and fit as ever! Be it body fat loss, lean muscle mass, muscle strength, or just plain conditioning, Craig's Turbulence Training is second to none. Thanks, Craig!"

Andy Apsay

"I started Turbulence Training at 210 pounds and 33% body fat, but after 12 weeks I'm down to 188 pounds and 21% body fat. I have lost 12% body fat which equates to a gain of 8 lbs. in lean body mass and a total loss of 30 lbs. fat. To say I'm pleased with the progress made is an understatement of unimaginable proportions. The progress I have made in 12 weeks has stunned me - I never knew I had it in me!"

Chris Curtis

"Thanks to Turbulence Training and Dr. Mohr's nutrition plan, I have finally been able to find a program that fit my lifestyle and allowed me to push my body fat below my comfort zone. In the past, I was using the popular exercise plans (I thought they were the only ones that worked), which were probably designed for steroid users. These five- or six-day, forty-five-minute to one hour workouts usually just led me to overtraining, missing a session, and eventually just quitting and looking for a new program. Nutritionally, I thought to get to low body fat levels I had to go ultra low carb and use all sorts of expensive supplements. This also was impossible for me to do.

"With Turbulence Training, I found workouts that took only thirty to forty-five minutes every other day, including cardio and with NO SUPPLEMENTS REQUIRED! 'Impossible,' I thought, but here I am twelve weeks later down almost twenty pounds and close to ten percent body fat."

Mark Russo

"Turbulence Training is a perfect fit for me! As a professional fire-fighter, physical conditioning is not only a job requirement but also a lifestyle that my life and the lives of others depend on. I used to go to the gym and focus primarily on strength training, one or two body parts a day, four to six days a week. Not only was I spending a lot of time away from my family, the workouts would leave me sore for days on end. When I realized that I was overtraining myself, I decided it was time for something new.

"That's when I discovered Turbulence Training. Within the first four weeks of your program I started noticing results. I was in pretty good shape when I bought your book, but TT makes me feel like a more well rounded fireman. No longer is cardio something I dread doing; with your interval training system I truly enjoy the end of each workout. And I'm spending only three days a week in the gym, which gives me more time with my family. Craig, thank you for putting a system together that is both efficient and functional."

Gabriel Refuerzo

"I am in week twenty-two of my Turbulence Training fitness regimen and I have been in love with it ever since I started the first week. I am doing TT workouts three times a week and playing tennis on at least two of my off days. I am 6'3", twenty-eight-year-old, and my starting weight/body fat percentage was 208/18.4%. I started with the 30-Day Fat Loss program, where I noticed results almost instantly. Diet had a lot to do with it as well. I have been following Dr. Mohr's plan and following the 90/10 rule, as my wife and I like to "throw down" on the weekends. During the week, though, my diet is strict, with lots of fruits/veggies (*lots* of broccoli), natural almonds in prepackaged snack sizes, and lots of chicken, turkey breast, and post workout protein shakes. After the four-week Fat Loss program, I dove into the Original

TT program. The mix of weight training with the high intensity intervals is the perfect fitness program. You are in and out of the gym in one hour and burn a ton of calories days after.

"Next I started the four-week bodyweight which I finished while on vacation in Jamaica. I really didn't believe it would be difficult until I started it. WOW, what a burn! I have continued the TT programs, 2k3 and am finishing up 2k4 this week. In these five months, I have upped my dumbbell press weight from sixties to seventy-fives. I can't wait to start 2K5 next week and see where I can get my bench up to. After twenty-two weeks of TT, I am now down to 190 pounds and 10.8 % body fat. I would still like to put on five pounds of muscle, but the way things are going, I know I can get there. Craig, thanks for the workouts, and keep 'em coming!"

Nick Walters

"I am a Melbourne, Australia-based personal trainer and martial arts instructor with many years experience in the industry. I have been using the TT programs and principles in my own training and that of my clients and have been very impressed with the results, as have they. My clients are training harder on briefer, more effective programs and are happy with the results to say the least. The training principles I've used for years have always been on the quality rather than quantity side, but the innovative program structuring that goes with TT is great and provides plenty of variety and challenge. Furthermore, from a personal perspective, my joints, which have been battered after years of martial arts and heavy weight training, are now more pain free and enable me to hit the gym and train hard and consistently. You have my full endorsement."

Sean Bowring
Zanshin Fitness Solutions

"Hi, Craig. You've done it again! You never cease to amaze me how you create your extremely effective fat loss Turbulence Training programs. My clients LOVE me, as I use your programs for my home-based training clients and they find them highly effective. In just eight weeks one of my female clients has dropped two dress sizes and fits into a pair of jeans that she had lost hope of ever fitting into again.

"Your TT programs are also wholly responsible for me getting back into shape. I started out at 82 kilograms and 24 percent fat. Six months later I am down to 75 kilograms and 15 percent fat. My clients are so happy with their results that they are all telling their friends, and I am getting more and more requests to help these women achieve the results their friends have! Thanks, Craig, I owe you big time."

Andy Wallis

"Craig, I just wanted to let you know that I've been using your Turbulence Training Workouts to whip myself back into shape after a vacation. I've dropped 10.2 lbs. of body fat in the last 28 days. As a fellow fitness professional I can safely say that it's the best and most efficient approach to improving body composition that I've come across."

Pat Rigsby

"This contest was exactly what I needed in my life to achieve the goals that I have been failing for the previous fifteen years. I have, probably like everyone else, tried and failed many times and never had the motivation to keep going. The accountability of knowing that I would be posting an 'after' photo kept my motivation high for the required intensity of the workouts and the mental focus needed to stay clean on my diet. Before TT I worked out at least three times longer and achieved less results. With the high intensity of the workouts coupled with the efficient design of the program, Craig has achieved a perfect balance for anyone, especially people with very little spare time. I will never spend more than one hour per day training again because I know that is all I need to achieve my physique goals.

"Going in, I knew that nutrition would be my biggest obstacle. Being overweight my entire life, I had finally come to the conclusion that I could not out train my diet. After cleaning out my kitchen and not having access to any of the foods that made me fat, changes started to appear immediately. Getting my body to relearn how to eat till I'm content, not stuffed, was the key to my success. Once I got into a routine, however, it became normal to eat that way. The cravings I used to have slowly disappeared, along with the fat. This is how I eat now, this is who I am. I will not go back to the old person I was, emotionally or physically.

"I kept it pretty simple and used the 2k3 for weeks one to four, 2k4 for weeks five to eight, and 2k5 for weeks nine to twelve. My strength levels stayed level throughout, which I was very happy about. As an adult I have never weighed below 160 pounds. Stepping on that scale yesterday and seeing 158.5 was awesome! My main goal was to see my abs. Although I didn't get totally ripped as I would have liked, I think that was more due to starting at a high BF% than to anything else. After a few weeks on maintenance, I intend to continue to implement the lessons learned during this contest to get to single digit BF levels.

"I just want to congratulate everyone who entered and thank everyone who helped me along. I especially want to thank Craig for designing this awesome program and sponsoring this life-changing contest. I'm in debt to you for life, man."

Adam Harper

Quick Reference Glossary

Baby-Step Method: Small, incremental gains in the pursuit of a larger, less-negotiable goal.

Calorie: Unit used to measure energy, more commonly associated with the potential energy of food products.

Cardio Confessional: Excessive exercise done in "penance" for previous day's diet.

Catecholamines: Hormones released by the adrenal glands in high stress situations. Generally associated with decrease in appetite and an increase in fat burning.

C.L.A.: Conjugated Linoleic Acid, a chemical derived from certain meats and dairy products, believed to have fat loss properties; but similar research and real world experience has negated previous findings.

Fat Burning Zone: Theory that there is an ideal heart rate for burning the maximum amount of fat. Considered by most to be a misrepresentation of the facts.

H.I.I.T.: High-Intensity Interval Training, an influential predecessor to Turbulence Training.

Life Applicable Fitness: A realistic exercise regiment that is sustainable as a long-term practice.

"Magic Bullet": The quick, typically easier solution to a problem but generally regarded as false or misleading.

Monounsaturated Fat: Healthy fat commonly found in nuts, seeds, and certain vegetables such as avocado.

Outcome Goal: Setting achievements without regard for how one will accomplish said goal. Example, "I will lose five pounds in one week."

Paralysis by Analysis: Indecision due to an abundance of information that is often contradictory.

Process Goal: Setting achievements that are directly affected by one's actions. Example, "I will go to the gym three times this week."

Reverse Goal Setting: Process that starts with the end point in mind, allowing for constant adjustment.

Saturated Fat: Unhealthy fat found in the typical "fatty" or "greasy" foods. Associated with heart disease and weight gain.

Subcutaneous Fat: Layer of fat above the muscle, typically soft, found on the back of arms, underneath the chin, and near the waist.

Super-set: A pair of exercises done sequentially with minimal rest between each. Example, pushups followed by chin-ups.

Visceral Fat: Fat underneath a layer of muscle. This is the hard, round, "beer belly" type fat, very unhealthy.

Chapter 12
Bodyweight Exercises: A Closer Look

Throughout the course of this book I've made numerous references to certain exercises. I described them briefly, but now I would like to revisit them for a better picture of what's actually happening. **Be careful!** These are not all beginner exercises and shouldn't really be used for instructional purposes. For that, you should consult TTMembers.com where you will find descriptions, pictures and videos of hundreds of exercises. What follows are simply a few how-tos so that what you read earlier will seem a little clearer.

Spiderman Push-up: Starting from a normal push-up position with hands parallel and palms flat to the ground, lower your body as you would for a regular push-up. Then pull your right knee up so that it swings alongside your body until it touches your elbow. Do not drag your feet! The balancing portion is half the exercise. After you have touched your elbow, do the same movement but in reverse back to the start of the push-up position. Alternate sides with each repetition. Remember: this is a slow movement with the leg and not a quick jerk.

Mountain Climbers: Starting from a normal push-up position with hands shoulder width apart, you want to keep your head up as you bring your right knee forward. Unlike the Spiderman push-up, for this exercise your knee will be passing underneath your body. When the knee cannot comfortably go forward anymore, tap the toe on the ground, and then retract the leg to starting position. Repeat this movement with the left leg. Also, unlike the Spiderman push-up, your speed for this exercise should be moderately quick but not to the point of poor form.

Pistol Squat: *This may be the most difficult exercise in the Turbulence Training arsenal. It is definitely NOT a beginner's exercise and only should be attempted with personal instruction.*

While standing on one leg, preferably away from any other objects, extend the non-weight bearing leg forward until it is parallel to the floor. With hands raised in front of your body to balance, lower yourself as if into a seat, or as you would for a regular weighted squat. When you are as low as you can safely go, contract your butt and thigh and return to the standing position.

Plank: At the complete opposite end of the Turbulence Training spectrum, there is the plank. The plank is designed to increase abdominal muscle endurance. Starting facedown, place elbows on the ground parallel to your shoulders. Then extend your feet directly behind you until your body is as straight as if you were standing up. Hold. Depending on what level of the program you are in this position may be held as long as two minutes.

Side Plank: Starting from your side on the ground, position your elbow at ninety degrees against the ground, almost as if you were leaning against a wall. With your feet on top of one another, lift your waist towards the ceiling until your legs, hips, and spine are straight. Hold. Due to the amount of weight on the elbow, you will find it more comfortable to do this on an exercise mat or carpet.

Inverted Row: This is one of the exercises that requires an adjustable chin-up bar, which unfortunately, is one of the only ways to exercise the upper back with just bodyweight. So, provided that you have an adjustable chin-up bar, position it in the doorway at hip height. Lie underneath the bar and grasp it with both arms extended and hands spaced two inches wider than shoulder's width apart. Then pull yourself up until your chest touches the bar. With squared elbows, slowly lower yourself.

Chapter 13
On the Net

As I've mentioned, the Internet has become one of Turbulence Training's greatest tools. Here is a list of sites to help you learn more and share with other people around the world.

- ✓ www.TurbulenceTraining.com/freegift
- ✓ www.TurbulenceTrainingForAbs.com
- ✓ www.TransformationContest.com
- ✓ www.TTMembers.com
- ✓ www.FitYummyMummy.com
- ✓ www.DietDebunker.com
- ✓ www.FitDay.com
- ✓ www.CalorieKing.com

Printed in the United States
132381LV00008B/10-21/P